TRADE TALKS

AHO, C. Michael. Trade talks: America better listen!, by C. Michael Aho and
   Jonathan David Aronson. Council on Foreign Relations, 1986 (c1985). 178p
   index 85-25559. 15.00 ISBN 0-87609-009-9; 8.95 pa ISBN 0-87609-010-2. HF 1721.
   CIP

The rising tide of protectionism worldwide has raised fears among many observers that
we may repeat the folly of the 1930s, when tariffs and other trade barriers caused a
catastrophic drop in world trade and incomes and contributed importantly to the
economic stresses that brought on WW II. In this book Aho and Aronson—both with
extensive experience with the US government in international affairs—set out the
problems and obstacles, plus the necessity, of a new round of negotiations aimed at
reducing trade barriers and stimulating the exchange of goods and services. Both the
economic and political shoals are explored, and the means of coping with them are laid
out. Special attention is given to the attitude of the major participants—the US, the
Economic Community, Japan, Canada, and the developing countries. As the authors
emphasize, the hurdles are formidable, but if we fail we could well see the dissolution of
the multilateral trading system and attendant economic chaos. Undergraduates and
general audiences.—E. Marcus, formerly Brooklyn College, CUNY

D1565099

TRADE TALKS

America Better Listen!

567374

C. MICHAEL AHO • JONATHAN DAVID ARONSON

Council on Foreign Relations

COUNCIL ON FOREIGN RELATIONS BOOKS

Library of Congress Cataloging-in-Publication Data
Aho, C. Michael, 1949–
  Trade talks.

  Includes index.
    1. Free trade and protection.   2. Foreign trade
regulation.   3. United States—Commercial policy.
I. Aronson, Jonathan David.   II. Title.
HF1721.A36   1986   382'.3'0973   85-25559
ISBN 0-87609-009-9
ISBN 0-87609-010-2 (pbk.)

To Amy and Joan

Contents

Foreword

Edmund T. Pratt, Jr.

The international trading system under the General Agreement on Tariffs and Trade (GATT) is at a critical juncture. Sluggish world economic growth, the oil shocks of the 1970s, and debt crises in some less developed countries, among other factors, have produced a return of world-wide economic nationalism that threatens to destroy the world trading system as we know it. One-by-one, nations have increased barriers to their domestic markets to protect local industries or to encourage the growth of new industries. One-by-one, they have adopted domestic industrial and economic policies, such as subsidies, that give their industrial and agriculture exports an unfair, favorable edge in world markets. Even the United States, the champion of an open international trading system in the post-World War II era, is engaged in a great national debate over the future direction of its trade policy.

It is clear to those of us engaged in international business on a day-to-day basis that the rules governing the world marketplace must be improved if we are to maintain fair and equitable access to international markets by exporting and investing abroad. If the GATT is allowed to weaken further, the resulting contraction in world trade not only could trigger a world-wide recession, but could well lower the standard of living of all peoples—including the American people.

In the months and years ahead, the nations of the free world— developed and developing nations alike—have a clear choice to make. They can either work together in the international interest to revitalize the world trading system under the GATT, or they can continue pursuing nationalistic economic policies that could well bring the system down.

Recognizing the great danger to the world trading system that we face, the United States has led the industrialized nations in calling for a new round of multilateral trade negotiations under the GATT. Unlike earlier rounds, the forces pushing us toward a new round in the 1980s are not simple questions of market access. Negotiating reductions of barriers to the free flow of trade—whether tariff or nontariff barriers—may no longer be sufficient to revitalize the international trading system. The GATT has become so unable to reconcile the differences between nations that we may have to negotiate a reform and strengthening of the GATT itself.

This book on the possible new GATT round addresses the issues surrounding the launching of negotiations. It clearly and concisely lays out the necessary agenda for negotiations, if the GATT is to survive, and identifies the major constraints to any new negotiations.

It is the first of several books to be published as part of the Council's work on its new international trade project, "The Future of the World Trading System and the Challenges for U.S. Trade Policy." Beginning in 1986, a series of volumes will examine in more depth many of the issues raised in this book, including the changing shape of global competition, exchange rates, trade in high-technology products, adjustment in basic industries, agricultural trade, services, the role of the developing countries in the trading system, and the future of U.S. trade policy. These books will be based upon a series of Council study groups to be held over the next three years.

In the meantime, the first volume provides a valuable assessment, for the concerned citizen as well as those engaged in the study of economic policy, of the immediate stakes we have in a new round of multilateral trade negotiations.

Edmund Pratt is Chairman and Chief Executive Officer of Pfizer Inc., and Chairman of the Steering Committee for the Council's international trade project.

Preface

The arms talks in Geneva have captured the imagination of the public. But now another set of talks is about to begin in Geneva which could also capture public attention. Trade talks (multilateral trade negotiations) resemble arms talks in important ways. Key terminology is identical: reciprocity, retaliation, escalation, threats, proliferation, concessions, commitment, credibility, transparency and verifiability. Other terminology is parallel. Trade negotiators talk of standstills and rollbacks; arms negotiators talk of freezes and build-downs. As tactics and strategy, unilateral reduction of trade barriers is about as likely as a unilateral reduction in armaments.

But the differences are striking as well. Comparisons between the balance of trade and the balance of terror can be easily overdrawn. Arms talks are at the heart of "high" foreign policy in which we are all either winners or losers. They are conducted by experts who are relatively unconstrained by domestic political considerations. Trade talks, when they are handled well, are "low" foreign policy. Trade negotiators (sometimes technocrats, but often politicians) are deeply constrained by domestic political considerations and influenced by pressure-group politics. Winners and losers are evident in each country, and the negotiations are as much domestic negotiations among affected interest groups as they are between countries.

But the trade talks are in danger of moving from "low" foreign policy to "high" policy. Trade is again on the front page of the leading newspapers: "U.S. Trade Deficit Could Exceed $150 Billion in 1985," "Reagan Fails to Secure Date For New Trade Talks at Bonn Summit," "Congress Awash in 300 Protectionist Bills," "U.S. Becomes Debtor Nation For the First Time Since 1914." And now, some trade tacticians in the United States are borrowing from arms terminology and talking about strategic intervention (to subsidize industries), compellent threats, reciprocity and retaliation. The United States is groping to find its way on trade policy, and the world is waiting nervously.

Although no longer as dominant, the United States is still looked to for leadership on international economic issues. Its

actions are emulated by others. After four years of largely ignoring
the international economy and the international economic consequences of its domestic economic program, the Reagan Administration appears to have changed course about 180 degrees on monetary
and exchange-rate issues and has finally attempted to articulate a
trade strategy. In the face of a Congressional threat to pass protectionist legislation, the Reagan Administration has accepted that the
strong dollar was causing many of the competitive problems facing
U.S. industry and has pledged to work with the other leading financial powers to bring it down. One other key component of their trade
strategy (and one that they have been pushing since 1982) is to
launch a new round of multilateral trade negotiations. Failing that,
the President has said that the United States stands ready to negotiate bilaterally and with like-minded countries. But the Congress
remains restive. Critical decisions lie ahead as the United States
decides what approach to take.

Will the United States abandon its traditional multilateral
approach to trade and adopt bilateral and regional agreements with
like-minded countries? Or will the United States adopt a tit-for-tat
aggressive trade policy, retaliating against alleged unfair trading
practices? Or will the United States turn inward, erecting, brick by
brick, a wall of trade restrictions, creating a fortress America? What
are the benefits and costs of these alternative approaches, and how
do they compare with a global bargain achieved through a multilateral negotiation? What tactics and strategies should be adopted to
affect the likely outcomes?

Slowly, U.S. policy makers are learning that trade policy can no
longer be ignored or treated as a stepchild of domestic economic
policy and foreign policy, and that America's competitive position in
the world economy should be accorded a higher priority among
government policies. Indeed, the cry from Capitol Hill and the private sector is for the government to articulate a trade policy. But the
only time the United States comes close to articulating a coherent
trade policy is in the midst of a major multilateral negotiation. A
new round of trade negotiations should begin in 1986. The Reagan
Administration's new efforts at international cooperation are just
what is needed to launch these talks successfully, but much more
will be needed to complete them.

This book is meant to provide policy makers, business executives, labor leaders and citizens in the United States and overseas
with an introduction to the issues, the players, the national objec-

tives, constraints, and strategies for these new trade talks. We hope this book is for trade what we would like to see written for arms talks—a primer for the interested, intelligent layman. Everyone has a stake in the outcome of these talks.

How did this book come about? The authors first met at the 1982 Ministerial Meeting of GATT. Although they were there as support staff, they had a first-hand view of the discord which characterized that meeting. Since then, both have been actively writing about, speaking on, and participating in the making of trade policy. Aronson concentrated on the new issues, working closely with scholars and business executives in the services sectors, particularly the telecommunications industry. He travelled to more than a dozen countries in 1985, analyzing developments in the telecommunications industry. Aho continued to work on adjustment issues and had an extraordinary opportunity to see the legislative process up close as the economic assistant to Senator Bill Bradley. While Aho was working for him, Senator Bradley participated in the GATT Wisemen's group assembled to study the problems afflicting the world trading system. This provided a remarkable vantage point. When the authors finally got back together in the spring of 1985, they decided that there was a need for a book on the problems and prospects for new multilateral trade negotiations. Each would bring his own relative expertise on issues and from professional training—one an economist, the other a political scientist. This volume is the result of that collaboration.

We are indebted to many people who helped at various stages in the production of this book. Tom Bayard, Geza Feketekuty, Joseph Greenwald, Gary Hufbauer, Abraham Katz, and Joan Spero participated in an authors' review group, ably chaired by William Diebold, to review a preliminary draft. We benefited a great deal from those discussions. Tom Atkinson, Peter Cowhey, John Leddy, Hal Malmgren, Irene Meister, David Munro, Alan Romberg, Dorothy Sobol, and Marina v.N. Whitman read the manuscript and made useful suggestions. We also received valuable comments from Myer Rashish on an abbreviated version of the text presented at a National Bureau of Economic Research Conference. The authors benefited from two meetings of the Steering Committee for the Council's International Trade Project, chaired by Edmund Pratt. Aho gathered significant insights at conferences with foreign experts in Aspen and Bellagio, and Aronson benefited from his participation in the European Communities' Visitors Program in May 1985. We are grateful to

General Motors and the Rockefeller Foundation for their generous support of the Council's trade project, from which this is the first publication.

Special thanks are due to William Diebold who read the manuscript repeatedly and engaged us in thought-provoking conversations and chaired as well the authors' review group. Paul Kreisberg, Director of Studies, also went through the manuscript twice and provided valuable feedback at various stages. David Kellogg as Publications Director and Robert Valkenier, our editor, are to be accorded special thanks. Without the benefit of their expertise and input, this book would have been delayed by months. Thanks are also due for the support given by Winston Lord and John Temple Swing, who headed the Council during the preparation of this book. In the final analysis, the book would not have been possible without the diligence and perseverance of Suzanne Hooper, Aho's assistant at the Council. She, more than anyone else, will be relieved to see this in print. Sue Roach, in the typing pool, also came through with a week's work during a critical three-day period. Finally, this book is dedicated to our wives, Amy and Joan, who read parts of the drafts, were supportive throughout, and make it all worthwhile.

> *C. Michael Aho*
> *Jonathan David Aronson*
> October 1985

Part I
Context

One

Introduction

The assembly of nations will shortly embark on a new round of multilateral trade negotiations under the auspices of the General Agreement on Tariffs and Trade (GATT). Pessimists question whether the time is auspicious for bold initiatives. The United States does not have its own house in order: the dollar is overvalued, the budget deficit looms large, and an economic downturn is likely. Support for new negotiations among traditional U.S. business proponents of freer trade is lukewarm at best. The halls of Congress, where enabling legislation must pass, echo with protectionist speeches. The Administration is still vague about what it hopes will emerge from the negotiations.

These problems bedevil the United States, the staunchest supporter of new negotiations. Other governments have even more doubts. Europe supports negotiations with an air of resignation, but with no visible enthusiasm. Japan favors multilateral negotiations because they will be long and complex and might divert attention from its bilateral trade tensions. The developing countries (LDCs), many saddled with serious debt problems, range in their views about new negotiations from skepticism to outright opposition. Few LDCs believe that they will get anything significant from a new multilateral exercise.

The trading system is in disarray. International cooperation is at its lowest point since World War II. With discipline lacking, a full scale trade war is a distinct possibility. Pressures for trade restrictions abound because of current unemployment problems and will increase because of the labor adjustment problems inherent in heightened international competition and in the transition from old to new technologies. Overvaluation of the dollar also increases the pressure for protection in the United States.

Yet, even as the trading system faces great dangers, opportunities are evident as well. The developing countries, the fastest growing markets for industrial country exports, still have vast pools of

3

unemployed or underutilized resources. Integrating the LDCs more fully into the trading system will be the greatest challenge of the coming decade. If this were to be accomplished, the world economy would get a sorely needed stimulus to growth comparable to the one the world enjoyed after World War II when the United States used its dominant economic power to promote trade liberalization in a series of trade negotiating rounds. For over a generation from 1950 to 1973, the world economy experienced unprecedented growth averaging 3.3 percent per annum. Trade liberalization was a major factor creating that growth and helped spread it around the world.

But those real income gains gave way to stagnation and unemployment in the mid-1970s. Now the trading system, from which all countries have benefited, is under severe pressure. Countries are pursuing more nationalistic trade policies and some are on the verge of adopting the beggar-thy-neighbor policies which characterized the Depression of the 1930s. In the words of the GATT "Wisemen's" group assembled to study the trading system, "Today the world market is not opening up; it is being choked by a growing accumulation of restrictive measures. Demands for protection are heard in every country, and from one industry after another."[1]

The case for free trade goes back to the eighteenth century and Adam Smith. As no two countries are alike in natural resources, labor force, terrain or climate, these differences give each country a "comparative advantage" over other countries in some products. If each country concentrates on producing goods in which it enjoys a comparative advantage and then trades with other countries for other products it needs, every country will be better off. Through trade, a country can obtain goods from the lowest-cost source of supply, and the competition from trade ensures an efficient domestic allocation of resources. When land, labor and capital are more efficiently employed because of trade, national and international growth increase. Almost all economists agree that aggregate welfare increases as trade is liberalized.

But trade is a complex policy issue, standing as it does at the intersection of foreign policy and domestic economic policy. Although nations as a whole gain from freer trade, the gains are net gains. Trade creates domestic conflicts of interest, even though freer trade increases overall income and welfare. Domestic adjustment is painful. Mobility is not perfect. Firms and their workers do not move effortlessly to sectors favored by comparative advantage. Together with community representatives, firms and workers adversely affected by import competition lobby their elected representatives to protect their interests. Politicians are easily tempted to buy political support from vocal minorities even if the overall good of the silent majority suffers. Producers' positions on freer trade depend upon whether they compete with imports or rely on foreign markets for sales or purchases. Consumers, who ultimately benefit from freer trade through lower prices and a wider variety of products, are not well organized or vocal in their support of freer trade.

The GATT system provides the rules and discipline under which trade is conducted. When that discipline is followed, uncertainty is reduced, which allows international investment, trade and growth to expand. Businesses can plan and invest on a global basis, and economies of large scale can be realized. However, considerations of national security and cultural sovereignty and protests by inefficient industries hinder progress toward freer trade. Some countries also actively intervene in their markets to support the development of their industries. GATT allows for exceptions, usually of limited duration, to enable countries to slow the pace of adjustment, but it does not adequately regulate policies used to accelerate the process of industrial development.

GATT was designed in the 1940s to deal with trade in goods because the exchange of goods dominated the world economy. Certain sectors such as energy and services were never covered by the GATT, and over time other sectors, prominently agriculture and textiles, became exceptions in the system. Although the GATT system changed considerably in response to new realities, the system has not kept pace with the rate of change in the world economy.

Why a New Round of Trade Talks?

Today the international trade rules embodied in the GATT are no longer adequate. A shrinking portion of world trade is covered by GATT and that portion is not handled very well. Governments no longer abide by, or even agree upon, the rules which should regulate trade. Important new actors and issues are not covered by the rules. In contrast to the earlier period, the trend in the trading system is toward fragmentation, not integration. New initiatives are needed to prevent further disintegration of the system. It is only a slight overstatement to say that the GATT has been overtaken by events. If present trends continue, it will not be an overstatement at all.

The United States is the demandeur for the new round, just as it has been the initiator of every postwar round of multilateral trade negotiations. This time, however, the U.S. economic juggernaut, while still the strongest in the world, is not as dominant. Throwing U.S. economic and political weight around will not wear others down and compel them to come to an agreement. Only cooperative solutions crafted to assure that all participants benefit will be negotiable and sustainable.

The Reagan Administration faces two dilemmas. First, at home, it can only obtain the necessary authority to negotiate from Congress by promising increased market access abroad. At the same time, other countries will only negotiate freer access to their markets if they believe that they will get something worthwhile from the United States. Credibly threatening to become protectionist may be enough for the United States to persuade others to negotiate. Accepting others' demands will be necessary to achieve progress once negotiations begin. But U.S. concessions will make it more difficult to obtain the authority to negotiate and to implement any agreement. So far, the United States has not signaled much about what it might accept; it has only put its agenda of demands on the table.

The Reagan Administration faces a second dilemma as it develops objectives for new negotiations. If the United States proceeds too far, other countries will accuse it of rigging negotiations for its own benefit, claiming that America has a secret plan which gives it an unfair advantage. But, without suggestions from other countries of what they want the round to accomplish, the Administration is attacked by Congress and some in the private sector as being unprepared for negotiations. Under U.S. law, the Administration cannot articulate specific objectives without input from formal private sector advisory groups. For their part, these groups have been unwilling to go on record until they are convinced that there is a strong likelihood the negotiations will be held and more information is available on what they will cover.

Fear of breakdown more than hope for breakthroughs has fueled advocates of a new round. The bicycle theory of negotiations is frequently cited: unless forward momentum is maintained, the trading system, like the bicyclist, will tumble over. The Administration claims that its primary goals are to strengthen, extend and revitalize the trading system. U.S. trade officials believe that it is essential to bring the trading system up to date to take into account growing internationalization and interdependence and to prepare to cope with the even more dramatic changes now under way.

Supporters of negotiations also see the entry into a new round as a way to block the increasingly protectionist demands voiced in every country. By focusing attention on strengthening trade rules, the Reagan Administration hopes to defuse a growing protectionist wave in the U.S. Congress as it stands poised to pass restrictionist trade legislation. The Administration's argument is that the best defense against protectionism is a strong offense for freer trade. It also hopes to bolster enthusiasm in the U.S. private sector, which has so far shown only qualified support for a new round.[2]

The issues which will frame the next round include the unfinished business of previous trade rounds, such as emergency import protection, subsidies and nontariff barrier codes; strengthening the trading system, by bringing sectors such as agriculture, textiles and steel back under the auspices of GATT; and extending GATT discipline to new areas such as services, high technology, investment, and intellectual property.

Current U.S. objectives center on strengthening the GATT as an institution and extending and reforming current international trade rules more than on trade liberalization. Other countries, particularly LDCs, put more emphasis on trade liberalization and a rollback of existing restrictions. Still others would rather talk about exchange rates, debt and the U.S. budget deficit.

The Dollar and the Debt Problems

Many observers overseas and in the United States feel international monetary reform is a more pressing issue than new trade negotiations. France has led the chorus arguing for multilateral talks on reform of the international monetary system, but the United States has resisted, agreeing only to a conference on a parallel track. Until mid-1985 the U.S. strategy was to allow some form of "alibi" discussions to defuse pressure. Although James Baker, the new Treasury Secretary, seems more willing to support parallel monetary discussions, it is questionable that such discussions will yield much, given the Reagan Administration's commitment to market forces and its opposition to macroeconomic coordination. (The U.S. Treasury has argued that official intervention could be swamped by billions of dollars of capital flows.) Nevertheless, those parallel talks should go forward because the problems are real and progress on trade problems will depend upon the solution to existing macroeconomic problems.

In September 1985 the prospect of some progress on exchange rates appeared on the horizon. As part of its strategy to counter the protectionist wave in Congress, the Reagan Administration enlisted the support of the other major financial countries (the United Kingdom, France, Germany, and Japan) to a coordinated effort to reduce the value of the dollar. After an unusual meeting in September 1985, the five agreed that "orderly appreciation of the main nondollar currencies against the dollar is desirable," and "they stand ready to cooperate more closely to encourage this."[3] What this will mean remains unclear, but recognition of the problem constitutes in itself a shift in policy by the Reagan Administration.

The overvaluation of the dollar has corroded the domestic consensus for trade liberalization in the United States. Some argue that dollar depreciation is a precondition for trade negotiations; but depreciation would reduce the willingness of others to negotiate. Europe is facing record unemployment and a depreciated dollar would increase the pressure there for restrictions. If anything, the overvalued dollar has helped to reduce political pressures for new trade restrictions there because European export industries have benefited from the overpriced U.S. products.

A parallel issue is the continuing debt crisis which substantially altered trade flows and taught the world that industrial and developing countries are all in the same boat. Several indebted developing countries are barely meeting their debt repayment schedules. A clear and important link exists between trade and finance. Unless LDCs can earn foreign exchange by selling their goods and services in developed countries, they will be unable to service their foreign debts and their growth prospects will collapse. If this happens, their ability to buy goods and services from industrial countries also will plummet. In consequence, although the financial problems of indebted countries will continue to be handled on a case-by-case basis and should not stand in the way of trade negotiations, debt issues will always be in view as these negotiations proceed.

Notwithstanding these macroeconomic and financial issues, a multitude of trade problems, many of which predate current macroeconomic circumstances, needs to be resolved. Although successful completion of the negotiations in a poor macroeconomic environment would be extremely difficult and macroeconomic issues will influence the pace and scope of negotiations, a poor macroeconomic environment should not stand in the way of launching negotiations which could take a decade to complete. True, the high dollar, U.S.

budget deficits, and the macroeconomic climate have to be addressed. But macroeconomic problems require macroeconomic, not trade, solutions. The internal ills of the trading system can and should be confronted on their own.[4]

We do not believe that U.S. efforts to bring down the dollar and reduce its budget deficits can or should be used as bargaining chips at trade negotiations. Necessary actions to correct the macroeconomic distortions which influence trade flows are desirable, but they are not trade concessions. Others will insist that the United States is responsible for making these corrections. It deserves no credit for carrying out its responsibilities. The same can be said for other countries.

How Change Comes About

The world economy evolves continually, usually in an incremental fashion. Over time, however, incremental changes totally transform the world system. Uncertainty and politics make it impossible for countries to revise rules and procedures often enough to keep the system relevant to the changing economic situation.

If at its start an international economic regime is strong and its goals and aims are clearly laid out, then the system may endure and prosper.[5] Eventually, however, the structure of the system and the reality of the economy it is meant to deal with diverge. Then the system needs an overhaul.

Change can come in a rush. After economic collapse, war, or revolution, major shifts often occur. At such times, short-term political differences can be overcome; major changes in direction become possible. For example, the World Bank, International Monetary Fund (IMF), and GATT emerged in the mid-to-late 1940s from the Great Depression and the rubble of World War II. The British and the United States governments believed that a complete restructuring of world economic rules was necessary to prevent a recurrence of the disorderly international economy of the 1930s. They triumphed even though none of the international institutions emerged as they envisioned them. Indeed, the GATT became the trade agency by default after governments failed to agree on an International Trade Organization with broader and more compulsory powers.[6]

Today, global economic interdependence assures that a severe shock or system disintegration would spread suffering everywhere.

Therefore, ways need to be developed to overhaul the system before the onset of economic adversity. The challenge is to make major adjustments before things fall apart.

Ideally, international economic regimes need to be developed that continue to evolve flexibly. National governments find this task extremely difficult. In international trade negotiations where domestic political considerations constrain every negotiator, such adaptive problem-solving is even harder. Even when all participants realize that adjustment is absolutely necessary, few politicians will sell out their constituents to benefit the whole. Generosity is even more difficult when there is no dominant leader willing to subsidize others to make the system stable. This is one reason why political leaders who have retired from the scene often call for major new international initiatives only after they no longer have the power to implement them.

We do not claim that new negotiations, entered without enthusiasm, will inevitably lead to a better system. One goal is to assess the constraints to adaptive reform of the trading system. Understanding these constraints may help find ways to overcome them. To this end, we first explore the economic and political situation underlying the need for reform. The precedents for change and a path to get negotiations started are then suggested. Our other goal is to examine possible outcomes in order to suggest what could be accomplished and what will make or break the negotiations.

Plan of the Book

In this volume, the trade negotiations are placed in a broad political context. The book addresses the benefits that trade negotiations could yield and examines the short- and longer-term interests of the key groups that will be involved in negotiations. Tradeoffs that will need to be accepted domestically and internationally to make a new trade round successful are emphasized.

The remainder of Part One sets the context and describes what could be accomplished. Apart from the decline in U.S. influence, which makes cooperative action imperative, several other factors will make these negotiations more difficult than earlier trade rounds. A larger number of countries will play a critical role in the negotiations. Growing interdependence makes the distinction between domestic and international policies obsolete. Sectoral and national distinctions are breaking down. The world has entered an era of higher unemployment and slower economic growth. Technological changes are transforming the industrial landscape, causing dramatic shifts in the composition of the labor force and creating additional adjustment problems. In short, the world is becoming more complex. Ten factors which will challenge trade negotiators are reviewed in detail in Chapter 2. Chapter 3 examines what the negotiations could accomplish—higher growth and greater discipline through expanded cooperation.

Part Two examines the self-interest of key participants in the coming negotiations. The American perspective is emphasized because the United States is the one most actively seeking negotiations and because its commitment is essential to launching and successfully completing a new round. We then turn to the interests of other industrial countries. Special attention is placed on the interests of the European Community and Japan, the other two pillars of the trading system, and on Canada. Finally, the economies of the developing world are considered. Distinctions are drawn between the Newly Industrialized Countries (NICs), the Organization of Petroleum Exporting Countries (OPEC) countries, high-debt countries, and the least developed countries. We also touch on the possible roles of China and Mexico in the forthcoming talks.

Part Three is more speculative. Too often policy analysts play it safe and explain only why things did not, do not, or will not work. We try to be more constructive. Chapter 7 discusses the advantages and pitfalls of bilateral and regional trade negotiations which could become prominent as a complement to multilateral negotiations or as a substitute for failed negotiations. Chapter 8 is more ambitious. It lays out an outline, not a detailed blueprint, of what we believe to be an economically sound and politically achievable package of reforms which, taken together, would constitute a major step toward revitalizing the trading system. We shape this package so that every country gains something and gives something by accepting what others want. Unless this type of a package is worked out, the outcome of negotiations almost certainly will be disappointing. If everybody gains, there is every prospect that significant progress can be made.[7] The last chapter assesses the outlook.

The reader may properly wonder if this book is written primarily as a guide for U.S. strategy in the round or, from a broader perspective, about the round and its possible contribution to improving the trading system. Our emphasis is on revitalizing the trading system. We examine what could be accomplished for the betterment of the global trading system, and what each country or groups of countries can contribute to that common objective.

A word on language is needed. Traditional language is inadequate for discussing trade negotiations. To trade negotiators, reducing trade barriers is considered a concession, even though economic theory teaches that unilateral reduction of trade barriers is in the national interest. However, in a political context, that is about as likely as unilateral disarmament. Trade barriers are part of the domestic rules of the game, and firms, workers and communities depend upon them and may be adversely affected if they are removed. Their interests must be and will be taken into account by elected officials. We follow standard negotiating practice and speak of import liberalization as a concession.

***

In summary, a major aim of the new trade round will be to forestall the collapse of the trading system. To succeed at anything beyond such damage control, the attitude of the negotiators must shift. Both a need and an opportunity exist to update and reinforce a trade structure that has benefited all nations over the past four decades. Off the record, officials from all countries agree that the trading system needs to be strengthened and updated and to become more flexible if it is to serve as a vehicle for continued international growth and prosperity. The challenge is to get from here to there without falling prey to the vagaries of national political necessity.

Each country has strong forces pushing it to protect its narrow interests and its most vocal interest groups. Yet, the system could collapse if it is torn apart by each nation pursuing its own short-term interest. The world is now so interdependent that it is impossible to isolate any economy from the whole. If protectionism replaces efforts to achieve freer trade, the effects will be felt everywhere. If the trading system crumbles, as it did under the weight of depression and protectionism in the early 1930s, no country will escape. In short, nations will either work together to revitalize the system now or pay the price if nationalistic trade policies bring the system down. It is useless to protest how difficult it will be to reach final agreement. The world economy will be different when these negotiations end. It is not yet the time to focus on what exactly will come out at the other end of these negotiations. For now, the task is to get things started down the right path.

Notes

1. See *Trade Policies for a Better Future: Proposals for Action*, GATT, March 1985, referred to throughout as the GATT Wisemen's report. A group of seven distinguished individuals were asked by the Director-General of GATT, Arthur Dunkel, in November 1983 to study the problems afflicting the trading system (not just GATT) and how they may be overcome in the future. They met over a period of seventeen months. The group, funded by outside sources, was independent of GATT and received input from a wide variety of sources. Dunkel did not attend all the meetings. The members of the group were Bill Bradley, United States Senator and member of the Senate Committee on Finance, and its Sub-Committee on International Trade; Pehr G. Gyllenhammer, Sweden, Chairman and Chief Executive Officer of AB Volvo and chairman of the informal Roundtable of European Industrialists; Guy Ladreit de Lacharriere, France, Vice President of the International Court of Justice; Fritz Leutwiler (Chairman), Switzerland, formerly Chairman of the Swiss National Bank and President of the Bank for International Settlements; Indraprasad G. Patel, India, Director of the London School of Economics and Political Science. Previously, he had been Governor of the Reserve Bank of India; Mario Henrique Simonsen, Brazil, Director of the Postgraduate School of Economics of the Getulio Vargas Foundation, formerly Minister of Finance and Minister of Planning of Brazil; Sumitro Djojohadikusomo, Indonesia, Professor of Economics at the University of Indonesia, formerly Minister of Trade and Industry, Minister of Finance, and Minister of State for Research of Indonesia. In Chapter 8 we review some of the wide-ranging recommendations for improving trade relations made by this group.

2. See "Chairmen's Report on A New Round of Multilateral Trade Negotiations," submitted to the United States Trade Representative, May 15, 1985. According to this report, "U.S. trade and economic policies are in desperate need of clarification . . . New multilateral negotiations alone . . . are incapable of dealing with the overall trade crisis."

3. *Communiqué of the Ministers and Governors of the Group of Five*, New York, September 22, 1985. See also the earlier *Communiqué of the Ministers and Governors of the Group of Ten*, Tokyo, June 21, 1985. Whether this will mean a major negotiation on the shape of the international monetary system remains to be seen. The annual meeting of the IMF and the World Bank in Seoul, South Korea, made no firm decision. More study was called for. In any event, the complexity of the problems makes that parallel negotiations on trade and monetary issues necessary. Otherwise, nothing might be done. Also, bringing financial issues into trade negotiations would bring in a whole new set of players and bureaucratic rivalries along with them. Moreover, in many countries, trade and finance ministers are rivals for higher office. Coordination would be difficult.

4. The Seoul meeting also made headway on debt and development problems after the United States indicated a willingness to increase the World Bank's resources for long-term structural adjustment loans and for concessional aid. For the most part, the linkages between trade and finance are omitted in what follows. However, some linkages are examined below, including restrictions for balance-of-payments reasons and coordination among the IMF, World Bank and GATT. Purely financial issues such as the form of international monetary arrangements are omitted. The whole subject of trade negotiations in itself is more than can be covered in a short book. Even some aspects of trade have had to be left out. Several trade issues are not discussed in this book either because they are tangentially related to the subject matter or are of less importance than those we have chosen to discuss. These include state-trading, the role of centrally planned economies in the GATT, countertrade and barter. Some of the earlier agree-

ments on licensing, customs valuation and product harmonization have also been omitted.

5. An economic system or regime may possess the equivalent of a corporate culture instilled by its originators that gives it life and purpose even after incremental changes begin to alter the system. Thomas J. Peters and Robert Waterman, *In Search of Excellence* (New York: Harper & Row, 1982), point out that an important aspect of corporate success is the corporate culture instilled by a dynamic founder. Once in place, a successful corporate culture lures others to share in it and continues to influence the direction of a firm long after the founder leaves the scene. Similarly, getting the culture for a new economic regime "right" may prolong its success and improve the likelihood that it can adapt to new, unanticipated challenges.

6. Richard Gardner, *Sterling-Dollar Diplomacy in Current Perspective*, (New York: Columbia University Press, 1980.)

7. One of the authors recently talked with a European official who pulled out the March 1985 report of the GATT Wisemen, *Trade Policies for a Better Future: Proposals for Action*, and commented, "On the record, of course, I must deplore this report because it would undermine some important European interests. Off the record, it is a good attempt to find a fair compromise with everybody giving something in exchange for what they get in return." The trick will be to make these private views acceptable in public.

Two

Setting the Context

The best way to begin devising recommendations for revitalizing the trading system would be to assume that no international trade rules were in place and that the GATT never existed. But rules, though imperfect, exist and influence behavior, positively and negatively. The present system must be taken as a point of departure.

GATT is one of the three major international institutions designed to help stabilize the world economy in the post World War II environment. But GATT does not have the authority in trade that the International Monetary Fund has in finance or the World Bank has in development. GATT is an administrative agency with a professional staff of fewer than 200 people. Its headquarters serves as a meeting place for participating countries (contracting parties) and houses negotiations when they are in progress.[1]

Over 35 years ago, in 1950, the United States balked at joining the more comprehensive International Trade Organization (ITO), because of business pressure and Congressional opposition to some of the ITO's authority. GATT was the portion of the ITO covering tariffs, which had already been accepted provisionally by the participating countries, and it became the international agency for trade, by default.[2]

GATT was born at a time when the memory of the Great Depression, characterized by international economic conflict, was firmly in mind. The world economy had seen the consequences of discrimination and retaliation in trade policies and did not like what it saw. Unfortunately, the experience of the 1930s is fading from the world's collective memory.

In the 1930s there was a turn toward sharply higher tariffs, quantitative restrictions, defensive economic alliances, bilateral deals, competitive devaluations, and subsidization of exports. After the passage of the Smoot-Hawley Tariff in the United States in 1930, trade spiraled downward, causing massive losses of jobs and output both directly and indirectly through a worsening of the financial crisis. Between 1929 and 1933, world trade fell by almost two-thirds. U.S. exports plunged from $5.2 billion in 1929 to $1.6 billion in 1933. U.S. imports fell from $4.4 billion in 1929 to $1.5 billion in 1933. Some three dozen governments formally protested the passage of the Smoot-Hawley Tariff. Within months of its signing into law, Spain, Switzerland, Canada, Italy, Cuba, Mexico, France, Australia, and New Zealand retaliated with new higher tariffs. Eventually 25 countries retaliated. Beggar-thy-neighbor policies spread everywhere and rival economic blocs emerged. The development of rival economic blocs not only contributed to the economic decline, but also played a major part in bringing on World War II.

Commenting on the relationship between trade policy in the 1930s and World War II, Richard Cooper described Herbert Hoover's signing of the Smoot-Hawley tariff as the

> most disastrous mistake any American President has ever made in international relations. . . . The sharp increase in American tariffs, the apparent indifference of the U.S. authorities to implications of their actions for foreigners, and the foreign retaliation that quickly followed, as threatened, helped convert what would have been otherwise a normal economic downturn into a major world depression. The sharp decline in foreign trade and economic activity in turn undermined the position of the moderates with respect to the nationalists in Japanese politics and paved the way for the electoral victory of the Nazis in Germany in 1932. Japan promptly invaded China in 1931. . . . The seeds of the Second World War, both in the Far East and in Europe, were sown by Hoover's signing of the Hawley-Smoot tariff.[3]

A number of lessons can be learned from the experience of the 1930s. It showed that retaliation and discrimination were the major elements behind the steep, world-wide growth of protection. It showed how difficult it becomes for businesses to bear the risks of trade-related investment when changes in the levels and forms of protection become less predictable. It demonstrated that heavy losses in output and employment occur when investment is reduced and directed into less rewarding projects. It showed that protection breeds protection, and that beggar-thy-neighbor policies are self-defeating because they end up by impoverishing all countries, especially the countries that practice them. Finally, it made clear that trade policy conflicts resulting in a decline in trade and output can provide fertile ground for political radicals to seize the reins of government. GATT's drafters wanted to protect against a repetition of these catastrophes.

The GATT was intended to help remove quotas and reduce tariffs and, to a lesser extent, other barriers to trade in goods through reciprocal trade agreements. The centerpiece of the GATT system (Article I) is the principle of unconditional "most-favored-nation" (MFN) treatment or nondiscrimination, which prohibits countries from playing favorites. In theory it works this way. Any trade advantage is automatically extended to all contracting parties and restrictions on imports are applied equally to imports from all sources. In the absence of discrimination, every contracting party can count on its exports to another signatory's market facing trade barriers no higher than those facing other foreign competitors. Bilateral trade treaties are not illegal, but any trade benefits given should be extended to everyone.

The GATT provided a process, complete with exceptions, escape clauses and enforcement mechanisms, whereby countries could move toward freer trade. Barriers to trade in goods have been reduced in seven rounds of multilateral negotiations since the 1940s. The GATT articles also prohibit trade restrictions other than tariffs except in strictly limited circumstances (such as acute balance-of-payments difficulty, when quantitative restrictions may be temporarily applied). This requirement is reinforced by rules about fair competition which allow countries to offset dumping and subsidization of goods coming from particular countries. Temporary "safeguard" increases in protection may be granted to industries injured by sudden surges in imports. Other procedures encourage countries to fix ("bind") the maximum levels of their tariffs, thereby reducing uncertainty about future tariff levels.

Originally, the most-favored-nation rule was qualified in just one important respect. Governments wishing to establish among themselves a single market embracing all products—a free trade area or customs union—are permitted to do so, even though this will inevitably involve giving better treatment to one another than to outsiders. A second, later, qualification permits the granting of preferences to developing countries.

In broad terms, the GATT system was built on a series of assumptions. (1) A multilateral framework is preferable to bilateral ones. (2) Unrestricted and nondiscriminatory trade will promote economic efficiency and growth in all trading countries. (3) If trade is conducted by private actors in competitive markets driven by supply and demand, efficiency and growth will be maximized. (4) Government intervention, which distorts the market, delays domestic adjustment and hampers growth and efficiency, should be avoided.[4]

In addition to nondiscrimination, the underlying principles of GATT included transparency and reciprocity. Trade-restricting actions were to be overt not covert, with prior notification and mechanisms for consultation spelled out. Reciprocity was a way to make trade negotiations politically acceptable. GATT is a bargaining arena where countries exchange concessions, but they are constrained by domestic interests. Bargains have to be acceptable to the diverse, conflicting interests represented within countries. Each country can decide what is in its national interest, seek that, bargain, and then "sell" the final negotiating package at home. In practice, particularly during the tariff negotiations, reciprocity meant that exports were considered a benefit and imports a cost. Negotiators seek greater market access for their exports; what is "given up" is greater market access for imports. Reciprocal bargaining works politically when exporters gain, even as import-competing interests experience pain and adjustment because of increased competition.

Historical Context: Successes and Disappointments

An examination of the GATT's evolution through its past successes and disappointments is instructive. The successes include the major rounds of negotiations (Kennedy and Tokyo) and the general sense of international obligations and responsibilities that the system has engendered. The disappointments include the exclusion of key sectors like agriculture and textiles from GATT disciplines and the 1982 Ministerial Meeting of the GATT.

Five rounds of tariff negotiations were conducted between 1947 and 1961, concluding with the Dillon Round in 1960-61. These negotiations lowered the average tariff from over 40 percent in 1947 to approximately 20 percent in 1961. The formation of the European Community (EC) in 1958 and increasing cold war tensions prompted the United States to push for new negotiations early in the Kennedy Administration. The Kennedy Round, launched in 1963, was more ambitious than previous tariff negotiations, included discussions on agriculture and antidumping practices, and took more than four years to complete. When it ended in June 1967, average tariffs were reduced by 36-39 percent. Little progress was made on agriculture and the antidumping agreement was not ratified by the U.S. Congress. Nonetheless, the Kennedy Round was hailed as a success in commercial relations.[5]

Work began almost immediately to identify, catalogue and analyze the remaining barriers to trade, particularly nontariff barriers. Several different organizations became involved, with a major report issued by the Organization for Economic Cooperation and Development (OECD) in 1972.[6] The United States began pushing for a new round of negotiations in 1970, but only after the collapse of the Bretton Woods monetary system did other countries agree to proceed. The imposition of the import surcharge in August 1971 by President Nixon and the possibility that the U.S. Congress might pass restrictive legislation worried other countries and persuaded them to agree to launch a negotiation at the Tokyo Ministerial Meeting in 1973.

The Tokyo Round proceeded slowly because the United States government did not obtain specific authority to negotiate until the end of 1974. The oil crisis, ensuing worldwide recession, and the U.S. presidential election campaign of 1976 also slowed progress. Most important, however, the need for further analysis and definition of the issues on nontariff barriers delayed progress. The subsidies discussions, for example, made little headway before late 1977.

After more than five years of negotiation, the Tokyo Round was successfully concluded in the spring of 1979. Tariffs were lowered by 27 percent to an average tariff level of under 5 percent. A new element was the signing of seven nontariff barrier agreements or codes. These codes established new discipline or liberalization in such areas as subsidies, standards, government procurement, customs valuation, licensing, and antidumping. They also established dispute settlement procedures and review committees to examine new issues that might arise. In this sense, they were meant to be the beginning, not the end, of the process. This was an encouraging sign because it suggested that GATT might become a more responsive, adaptive trade policy organization which could address issues on a continuous basis. It has not worked out that way, in part because of the limited number of countries which have subscribed to the codes and in part because some of the rules were left deliberately fuzzy where countries could not agree on which practices should be ended.[7] By mid-1985, six years after the round ended, the standards code had 33 signatories, the government procurement code 21, and the subsidies code only 19. Nonetheless, the conventional wisdom is that the Tokyo Round also was a successful endeavor in commercial relations.[8]

The success of GATT also contributed to more harmonious

international political relations. Since the GATT was founded, there has been no world war and today war between France and Germany is virtually unimaginable. Furthermore, democratic values are taking root throughout Europe, even in Spain and Portugal.[9] It is difficult to distribute credit for these successes between the GATT, the Marshall Plan, the formation of the European Community, NATO, and the use of active macroeconomic policy to avoid the disastrous economic slumps of earlier periods. In any event, harmonious trade policy allowed other issues to occupy the attention of foreign policy makers. In that way, GATT played a critical, although largely unseen and unappreciated, role.

The disappointments have been chronicled by numerous authors.[10] Agriculture and textiles are addressed in the next chapter. For our purposes the most recent disappointment is perhaps the most instructive. The 1982 Ministerial Meeting, the first in nine years, was held in the middle of a worldwide recession, a poor time to strengthen international cooperation. It suffered because it tried to do too much without any clear consensus about what needed to be done. Although preparations began almost a year in advance, there were still a multitude of disagreements to be resolved when the ministers arrived in Geneva (i.e., the draft communiqué was laden with bracketed language).

Almost all previous GATT Ministerials were used to launch new rounds. This time the United States, in its role as an initiator, backed off from that goal even before the meeting began. Furthermore, the two political "bottom line" issues for the United States—agriculture and services—did not lend themselves to a single negotiation because the European Community opposed agriculture and the developing countries opposed services. A triangular negotiation developed, and William Brock, the U.S. Trade Representative, was exasperated and ultimately exhausted as the Community and the developing countries took turns adjourning to caucus. The Ministerial concluded almost two days late despite round-the-clock sessions over the last four nights.

The results of the Ministerial Meeting were meager. There were no major breakthroughs. Dispute-settlement procedures were refined. Principles covering import relief as a safeguard protection were enunciated, but additional negotiations were scheduled. An agricultural committee was established. It was agreed that services, counterfeiting, textiles and exchange rates should be studied further. Agreement was reached to review the Tokyo Round nontariff barrier codes to determine their adequacy. Trade-distorting investment practices and trade in high-technology products were dropped. Its greatest success was that before the ministers limped home, they reaffirmed their commitment to GATT principles and practices.

Since 1982, however, new and extended bilateral circumventions have further undermined confidence in the system. No country is without sin. The United States has negotiated auto agreements with Japan and steel agreements with over a dozen countries. The EC implemented overt agreements in steel and more subtle arrangements in autos and electronic equipment. Japan, the major target of many of these bilateral restraints, accepted them voluntarily. Brazil's informatics policy, which excludes foreign computer producers, is but one example of increasing protectionism among the LDCs. These circumventions hurt the system, distorting trade flows and establishing precedents for similar action at a later date.

Still, since November 1982, countries have inched toward a new trade round. The debt situation and the high dollar slowed progress, but the U.S. economic recovery and the mounting U.S. trade deficit spurred on U.S. government efforts. The U.S. government worked hard to persuade its Quadrilateral partners (the European Community, Japan and Canada) to initiate a new round and began to address LDC doubts with positive arguments instead of rhetoric.

Small steps toward preparation were started. The beginning of discussion among industrial countries in the 24-nation OECD helped define what might be taken up in new trade talks. The GATT moved more slowly. The LDCs delayed the ability of the GATT Secretariat to address new issues until early 1984 when discussions of national studies on trade in services that were mandated at the 1982 Ministerial began.

The U.S. government pressed on. Ambassador Brock insisted that the United States would negotiate to liberalize trade. If the LDCs or recalcitrant industrial countries blocked negotiations under the GATT, the United States would negotiate bilaterally or with smaller groups of like-minded countries. It indicated that any results of these talks would be extended to only those countries which accepted the discipline and participated in the give-and-take of negotiations.

Japan and Canada supported efforts to begin a new round quite early in the process. In March 1985 the European Communities added their endorsement. By the spring of 1985 some of the developing countries, particularly the Asian NICs, were becoming more inclined toward new negotiations, even though India and Brazil continued to oppose them vigorously.

President Reagan and his top advisers hoped that the Bonn Summit, in May 1985, would put the industrial leaders on record as favoring negotiations and set a 1986 date for them to start. The French balked at setting a firm date. (Some regarded this as the first French posturing of the new round, not as a sign that it might not proceed.) In June, progress toward setting up the round took a step forward when ministers from 22 countries meeting in Stockholm agreed to submit papers describing their national goals and objectives to the GATT in July and that senior officials would meet in September to continue the process of preparation.[11] (The statement of U.S. objectives for a new trade round appears as Appendix I; the European Community statement of March 1985 as Appendix II.)

The GATT Council meeting in July proved more contentious. Brazil and India remained adamantly opposed to new negotiations and received support from a few other LDCs. In frustration, the United States, Canada, Japan, and the EC tried to hasten the official start of negotiations by resorting to the little-used GATT Article XV to call for a meeting of the contracting parties in September. Sixty-one of the contracting parties, fifteen more than the simple majority required, voted for the meeting. (That a poll was needed in an organization governed by consensus indicates how deep the differences of opinion are.)

At the September meeting Brazil, India, Argentina, Yugoslavia, and Egypt continued to oppose inclusion of services in a new round. But the contracting parties unanimously agreed to begin to prepare for a new round by setting up a committee that is to report to the annual meeting of GATT in November. They agreed that the committee must not "prejudge" the question of services, but the new round must assure that GATT is responsive to "changes in the trading environment." Clearly, disagreements over agenda remain, but as Arthur Dunkel, the Director-General of GATT, put it, "there are bloody battles ahead, but the debate is no longer over procedure—it is over the substance of the negotiation." The November meeting will likely establish a formal preparatory committee to work out timing and agenda.

How soon the negotiations will begin depends upon the tradeoff between wanting as many countries as possible to participate and wanting to avoid lengthy delays in starting the negotiations. To be truly multilateral, the major developing countries will have to agree to participate. Ultimately, they will join the negotiations when disagreements over the agenda are resolved. Otherwise, the industrial countries will start without them. Talks could begin by the summer of 1986.

The environment for new talks is difficult. Steel, autos, textiles, apparel, footwear, and telecommunications are just a few of the sectoral hot spots. The 1984 U.S. bilateral deficit of $37 billion with Japan is an obvious source of friction, but the United States has larger deficits on a per capita basis with Canada and Taiwan. Disputes among trading partners over specific policies are neither new nor particularly worrisome. What is unusual and troublesome about trade problems today is that they escalate quickly into highly politicized issues involving "zero-sum" diplomacy. Increasingly, trade policy is viewed as a strategic game in which national economic gains can only be reaped at another's expense. This view is in sharp contrast to the postwar perspective that freer trade provided mutual gains to trading partners.

Trade creates difficult policy problems for decision makers and elected officials because of the diversity of interests which are affected. The consequences of the increased import competition are concentrated in specific sectors and are felt immediately, and the affected firms, workers and communities quickly complain to policy makers. Consumers benefit from a wider variety of products and lower prices, but these benefits are diffuse, largely unseen, and are often felt over time. Exporters gain from greater foreign access, but they usually do not actively intervene in trade policy issues that do not directly affect them. Importers and retailers have a more direct stake, but their numbers are few. The challenge facing policy makers is to balance continually these diverse interests.

In the face of these challenges, progress is necessary to begin to restore confidence in the fairness and efficacy of the trading system. There is a fundamental asymmetry in trade policy formulation because the benefits of protection are concentrated and the costs are diffuse. Only when the protective structure is examined as a whole, in the context of a major round of negotiations, do the diffuse gains for the nation from trade liberalization become large enough for the political process to resist new restrictions. Therefore proponents argue that, as in the past, negotiations are needed to provide a way for organizing the political will to push the trading system forward. Ongoing negotiations give policymakers and legislators something to point to in resisting the requests of special interests for protection. Only in the context of a major round of negotiations do affected private interests favoring freer trade mobilize and lobby effectively. (Some analysts go so far as to suggest that permanent negotiations would be a good idea.)[12]

The question remains: would a new round raise unattainable expectations? If so, such an effort could be counterproductive. Failure might undermine existing arrangements, which still make important contributions to orderly international transactions. The political disagreements among countries outlined above will influence national positions and contribute to the discord as the negotiations proceed. But more fundamental economic forces at work will complicate the negotiations as well. The next section explores the underlying factors that will make progress difficult to obtain.

Ten Policy Challenges: Why These Negotiations Will Be Different and More Difficult

The coming negotiations will be more difficult, more complicated, and probably longer than any that preceded them. At least ten significant developments will challenge the ingenuity and determination of government leaders and their negotiators.

First, the *world has become more interdependent*. The integration and interdependence of separate national economies in a unified global economy have made them much more sensitive to foreign interventions and rendered the distinction between domestic and foreign economic policies almost meaningless. There no longer are purely domestic economic policies. Internal conditions or policies in individual economies are quickly transmitted across national borders through trade, technology and financial flows. Ostensibly "domestic" policies directed at taxes, agriculture, regional development, or investment have as much impact on international trade flows as tariffs or quotas. U.S. domestic economic policies, whether microeconomic or macroeconomic, have a significant influence on the domestic economies of its trading partners. The reverse is also true. Borders have become fuzzy and permeable.

Attempts to deal with the trade effects of interdependence are often viewed as infringements on sovereignty and then quickly become politicized. If the microeconomic "domestic" policies of one country injure firms and workers in another country, the second country promptly claims unfairness and demands redress. Worse still, there is no multilateral agreement on which practices are fair and which are not. The definition of unfairness has become a central trade policy problem. In the absence of a multilateral agreement, national politicians are unilaterally defining unfair trade practices (as the U.S. Congress has done periodically in revising unfair trade practices statutes), and these unilateral definitions are inconsistent with one another.

Furthermore, trade, monetary, investment, and foreign aid policies can no longer be compartmentalized. For practical, tactical, or political reasons, the U.S. government is trying to isolate trade negotiations from monetary issues while linking them to investment issues. Others prefer to link trade and monetary issues, but isolate investment ones. In any event, what happens in one forum will inevitably affect what happens elsewhere. Nonetheless, the conceptual and practical problems of trying to deal with all of these economic issues simultaneously are so great that trying to do everything at once would probably mean that nothing would get done. The best way to make progress on trade issues is to treat them separately even though what happens with trade will influence monetary, debt, and investment practices, and vice versa. Afterwards, the consequences of trade reforms can be dealt with in other parts of the economy.

In short, growing interdependence blurs boundaries, both national and conceptual. Distinctions and data are not as clear as they once were. Negotiations, therefore, will be more difficult.

Second, relative *U.S. dominance has declined*. Even though the United States is still the strongest economy in the world, it can no longer defend the open trading system alone. In the early postwar period the United States accounted for a large share of world trade, but trade itself was a relatively unimportant component of total U.S. output. In 1960, for example, the United States accounted for 16 percent of total world exports and 24 percent of industrial-country exports, while exports of goods and services were only about 6 percent of U.S. gross national product (GNP). In the 1970s the United States' share of world trade declined, while the share of trade in American GNP rose. By 1980 the American share of total world exports fell to 11 percent, the American share of industrial-country exports declined to 17 percent and American exports grew to 13 percent of GNP. Japan, Europe, and the developing countries have all gained on the United States. Today, the United States can no longer dominate negotiations, and more cooperation is required.

Even if it still could dictate economic terms to the rest of the world, the United States is no longer willing to lead alone. International economic integration has provoked a strong domestic reaction. Domestic political forces have mobilized to resist internationally induced change as never before.[13] The United States can still flex its economic muscles to further its own ends, but domestic constraints impair its ability to liberalize trade without clear reciprocal actions by other countries. When trade played a relatively small role in the American economy, it was easier for the government to overcome the domestic opponents of trade liberalization. As the importance of trade has grown, it has become increasingly difficult for policy makers in the United States to achieve a strong domestic consensus in support of trade liberalization. These trends are likely to continue. In the United States, generosity has waned and the determination that every country should pay its fair share has increased.

The decline in the ability and will of the United States to lead is disturbing. History shows that it is easier to establish and maintain free trade if there is a dominant country willing to accept the burdens as well as the benefits of leadership.[14] Although a few key countries working together with careful attention to the needs of other, smaller participants can keep things running smoothly, successful joint management of any individual issue like trade requires explicit acceptance by key countries that multilateral cooperation is needed and desirable.

Today, there is a special need to build international coordination and cooperation because no single country is likely to dominate the international economy again anytime soon. The European Community (EC) has a combined GNP and volume of trade comparable to the United States. Japan is closing the gap and ranks as the third pillar. Although the EC and Japan have an abiding interest and commitment to the principle of free trade, they have not taken the lead in defending it. Joint leadership is necessary, particularly because growing flirtations with unilateralism threaten to undercut present efforts at multilateral cooperation. However, even when established, joint leadership is less stable and more prone to delay than a regime characterized by a single hegemonic leader.

Third, a related development which complicates decision making is the *increased pluralism in the trading system*. More countries will play a critical role in the negotiations. GATT had 22 original signatories. Today, 90 countries are full signatories and 30 more apply its rules, de facto. Although the role of new actors such as the newly industrialized countries (NICs), the members of OPEC, and China is growing in international trade, they have no deep-rooted commitment to free markets.

Bargaining diplomacy has replaced power diplomacy as the mode of operation. But the trading system's rules and procedures are public goods. Public goods are those which, once provided, it is impossible to limit access to or get payment from new subscribers. They can be free riders. In a bargaining context, it pays for each country to understate the benefits it receives from the system. This greatly complicates the negotiations unless new means are found to put pressure on free riders and foot draggers.

Fourth, the world has entered an era of *slower economic growth and higher unemployment*. Adjustments to changes in trade or trade liberalization are easier when economies are expanding and unemployment is low, for growth is a lubricant which smoothes adjustment problems. Policies which may result in worker layoffs are more likely to be resisted in a stagnant economy.[15]

In the OECD area, growth rates have decreased and unemployment rates have increased over time. The OECD unemployment rate when the Kennedy Round was completed in 1967 was about 3 percent; growth was proceeding at an annual rate of over 5 percent. When the Tokyo Round ended in 1979, the unemployment rate was 5 percent and growth was 4 percent. Today, unemployment is 8.5 percent (over 11 percent in Europe) and growth is under 3 percent (only 2 percent in Europe).

The future does not look much better. The economic outlook is for continued slow growth, under 3 percent through 1986 with unemployment rising slightly.[16] The pace of structural change will not slacken and could accelerate during the rest of the 1980s and in the 1990s. The fundamental long-term changes occurring in the structure and operation of the world economy heighten the need for flexible and efficient adjustment to economic change. But these changes are coming at a time when, at least in some countries, the processes of adaptation have slowed down and the backlog of accumulated obstacles to change is severely hampering economic performance. Political resistance to change spills over into domestic and international conflicts on trade and trade policy. Labor adjustment problems are likely to be a paramount political problem for the remainder of the century.

Technological advance is reshaping national economies, but in many countries it has not led to much net job creation. In all countries manufacturing employment is declining, while service employment is expanding. The large number of jobs being created is being offset by the job losses elsewhere in the economy.[17] Where significant displacements are occurring, workers and their elected representatives hesitate to support policy changes, like trade liberalization, which could lead to more displacements. Concessions are always easier to make when the economic pie is growing and employment is expanding than when they are not.

Policy makers, however, often forget that the relationship between growth and adjustment runs both ways: growth eases the adjustment process, but adjustment is essential to growth. Maintaining flexibility, particularly in labor markets, is a key to increasing growth in the future. Countries that make the necessary adjustment to structural change will enjoy greater economic progress. Too often, however, government interventions to protect industries impede labor market mobility and adjustment and undermine the open trading system. The conflict between the need for economic adjustment to increase growth and the political pressure to erect obstacles to adjustment will continue and probably intensify in the future.[18] As different countries decide whether and how much to intervene, the task of negotiating trade liberalization grows harder.

Fifth, *the easy things have all been done.* New types of barriers will be the focus of efforts to liberalize in the coming trade talks. Except for politically sensitive industries like textiles, tariffs have been reduced significantly during the previous seven negotiations. The average tariff was lowered from over 40 percent in 1947 to 5 percent today. Those negotiations were relatively straightforward because tariffs are transparent and easy for policy makers to follow and understand. But success in reducing tariff barriers has spawned new problems. There are two schools of thought. One view is that as tariffs were lowered nontariff barriers (NTB) that had always existed but never much mattered became apparent. Many such barriers protected and promoted social, cultural, and security interests, but, intentionally or not, they also curtailed trade. The other view is that as soon as tariffs fell, countries devised new ways to protect national interests and interest groups. The truth falls somewhere in between.

These new obstacles hampering international trade are just as effective at preventing imports, less transparent, and more difficult to persuade countries to remove. Indeed, nontariff barriers, particularly those aimed at the service sectors, may actually be more restrictive than tariffs on specific goods. Many nontariff barriers on products and services are opaque and their restrictiveness is more difficult to judge. By limiting and distorting foreign access to domestic transportation, financial, and telecommunication infrastructures, nontariff barriers may retard imports across a wide range of goods and services.

GATT rules on subsidies and other NTBs are not as explicit or as fully accepted as the rules on tariffs. Although the Tokyo Round did address NTBs in a series of codes, they have been found wanting, particularly the subsidy code. When a country feels damaged by another country's subsidies, it claims unfair trade, retaliates and resists further reduction of its own trade barriers. But to proceed in this fashion undermines the GATT system. Improving coverage of NTBs will be central to the new talks.

Sixth, *excess capacity* is a growing problem. In sector after sector, the world can grow, build, and produce more than it can sell, deliver, and consume. The challenge is to allocate production and to assure distribution. Markets could do both, if only governments would let them.

Developing countries eager to industrialize insist that they must have textile, steel, and chemical industries. A striking example is that when the tiny Arab Emirates found themselves awash in a sea of petrodollars, they each insisted on building ethanol refineries as the first stage in their plans to integrate vertically, and each also wanted a world-class port and airport. Today, the ethanol plants are unbuilt or underutilized and none of the ports and airports runs economically. Any country with the capacity to buy or run automobile, airplane, construction or electronics industries wants them. Meanwhile, industrial countries are intervening to protect basic industries which suffer from global excess capacity. GATT has not been able to address the problems of excess capacity on a multilateral basis as countries have resorted increasingly to bilateral restrictions outside of GATT. The logical conclusion of this trend is a cartelization of industry.

Seventh, today many countries are using *industrial policies to create competitive advantage* for their industries. In this rapidly changing world economy in which technological advance can alter the conditions of competition almost overnight, alternative theories of trade based upon learning curves and dynamic economies of scale have been gaining wider acceptance. These theories stress government intervention and commitment and have little in common with the traditional factor-endowment theory.[19] Japan, France, and several

LDCs have instituted policies to foster technologically advanced industries. Even Brazil, far in debt and struggling to make its agriculture and basic manufacturing industry competitive, insists on devoting scarce financial and human resources to developing an informatics industry. The United States officially deplores such industrial policies, but its heavy spending in the security area is an indirect form of industrial policy.

U.S. efforts to focus GATT negotiations on rules for high-technology trade are aimed in part at these industrial policy issues. Just as every country cannot run balance-of-payments surpluses every year, every country cannot continually increase its share in every vital old or new sector. If every country insists on developing almost the same group of industries, the result will be excess capacity and trade conflict. Unfortunately, there is no agreement on what constitutes legitimate support for the development of an industry. Explicit subsidies can be countervailed against, but government procurement policies and subsidies for research and development (R&D) at the outset of industrial development can bestow advantages which last for years. In the absence of a multilateral agreement on which policies are acceptable, internationally inconsistent industrial policies will heighten trade conflict.

Eighth, *sectoral distinctions are breaking down*. For example, financial supermarkets are replacing separate banking, insurance, brokerage, and securities industries. Similarly, the merging telecommunication, computer, and broadcasting technologies are creating a new world information economy. The blurring of sectoral lines discourages the development of a clear plan for negotiating agreements on trade in services. Actually, the complications are greater.

The information and service input into manufactured products is increasing. In addition, many manufacturing firms find that a growing percentage of their revenues and profits comes from services they sell in association with products they produce or independent of them. According to computer manufacturers, a decade ago the value of a computer was attributed about 80 percent to hardware and 20 percent to software development. Today, those percentages are reversed. Manufacturers of digital communications switches—the heart of any phone system—report that the same trend is evident in the development of new switches. When 80 percent of the cost of development and manufacture of a computer or switch involves programming and other services, how should such products be dealt with in a trade context? Trade negotiators will have to accept and learn to deal with even greater complexity.

A ninth development, ignored to date by trade negotiators, is how to respond to the *changing shape of global competition*. Firms from different countries are forging complex alliances across sectors. Joint venture strategies and cooperative arrangements have divided the world market among coalitions of competing, internationally based alliances.[20] These international alliances may share the work in the development, production and marketing of goods and services in ways that have little to do with traditional models of trade. For example, transfer prices do not reflect arms-length transactions across national boundaries. What's more, many of the transactions do not cross borders in the traditional way, but instead are carried over telephone lines or beamed by satellites. Another example is that European firms prefer alliances with companies from America and Japan to associations with other European firms.

Multinational corporations are planning and operating on a global basis as negotiators continue to view the world in terms of competing economies. The discontinuity between the way corporations see the world and the way governments are structured to deal with trade problems is widening. Shifts in the shape of competition demand revisions of trade rules and principles during the coming trade round. Negotiations are traditionally conducted on a most-favored-nation basis among at least a subset of the world's economies. Although the participating nations may not discriminate among themselves, firms can and do establish preferential arrangements with individual countries. This can lessen competition and distort trade. Unless negotiators are flexible enough to recognize and react to this, negotiations may create rules that will be out of date before they are put in place.

This raises questions about the role of multinational firms in supporting efforts to liberalize trade. Historically, they were major supporters of trade liberalization, but they may be less supportive now. Firms which plan on a global basis may want strictly enforced international rules because that would reduce the uncertainty and the cost of doing business. But corporations grandfathered in countries behind trade barriers or investment distortions benefit from them.[21] In some cases, existing restrictions serve as barriers to entry to potential competitors and allow the firms to make oligopoly profits. To remove the restrictions would change the rules of the game. For these reasons, multinational firms may be more enthusi-

astic about a standstill on trade restrictions than about a rollback of
existing restrictions.

A tenth complicating factor is *time*. In many areas the time
between the introduction of new generations of products and services has shortened. For example, the standard black telephone
existed unchanged for decades. Today, new phones and phone services are introduced in quick succession. Similarly, the introduction
of cheaper, faster, and more powerful computers and computer
equipment is an almost monthly affair. No sensible purchasers of
micro- or mini-computers would buy the same thing today as they
did two years ago. As a result, the shape of competition in the world
economy is changing at a faster and faster pace. This means that
negotiators will need to make sure that the results of prolonged
negotiations are relevant to the world economy that is coming, not
just the one that exists today.

The lesson underscored by these ten developments is that the
world trading system and the world economy are likely to diverge
from the rules of the system faster in the future than in the past.
Unless more flexible ways are found to update rules, the coming
trade negotiations will solve little and may even hamper the ongoing
world-wide economic adjustment process. These negotiations
could last a decade. What is needed is a way for negotiators to incor-
porate what they learn as they proceed in the negotiations. Greater
reliance will have to be put on establishing ongoing processes and
procedures which can examine new developments as they arise in
order to assess their importance and policy implications. A protracted negotiation is also the best reason to begin now, because the
longer we delay, the further behind we will fall.

* * *

The picture that we paint is fairly bleak. The threat to the system
today is more serious than the periodic shocks and crises of the past,
precisely because the deterioration is gradual, less perceptible, and
not amenable to a "quick fix" or a one-shot change in the rules.
Long-run trends which portend slower growth, but with more pressures to adjust output and employment, give rise to policy interventions which directly or indirectly distort trade flows and further
inhibit growth and adjustment. Many view international trade as a
zero-sum game in which trade policy can be used to alleviate domestic problems temporarily. If interventions spread and intensify

within individual countries and provoke retaliation abroad, trade will change from a positive-sum game to a negative-sum game. The inability of the existing institutional framework to come to grips with these issues erodes its credibility and further weakens the trading system.

How can the world trading system move forward? A new round of trade negotiations could be the medicine needed to restore confidence in the trading system and to re-emphasize that trade liberalization is a positive-sum game. GATT is a mirror that reflects the cooperation that governments put into it. During major rounds of negotiations that cooperation is at its highest level. But, many problems afflict the trading system and everything cannot be done in the context of a new round. Priorities must be established.

What should the new round emphasize? Questions abound. How much should be done to shore up the deteriorating foundation of GATT? Should GATT be expanded to cover new activities and practices not covered adequately by existing rules? How much emphasis should be put on integrating the developing countries more fully into the GATT system? What institutional changes could be made to improve trade relations and make the system more responsive to emerging problems? Finally, can and should the GATT system be made more rule-oriented, embodying greater discipline and more clearly articulated procedures? Above all else, the negotiations must focus on the mutual gains from higher growth and must strengthen the discipline and cooperation in the system.

Notes

1. By comparison, the IMF has approximately 1,700 employees and the World Bank over 6,000. The tenuous status of the GATT Secretariat is perhaps best exemplified by its formal status. It is the Secretariat of the Interim Committee for the International Trade Organization; an organization which has been defunct since 1950. Even today the Secretariat's identity cards for use in Geneva bear the inscription of this defunct organization. The U.S. contribution to the GATT budget is approximately $3 million out of a total budget of $21 million in 1984 which is smaller than the U.S. contribution to almost all other international organizations, even the most minor.

2. It is of some interest that the ITO was formulated at the U.N. Conference on Trade *and* Employment. The ITO grew out of concern that the postwar trading environment should avoid a repetition of the economic disorder of the 1920s and 1930s caused by beggar-thy-neighbor policies designed to shift the burden of unemployment onto others. For a description of the disposition of the ITO in the United States, see William Diebold, "The End of the ITO," Princeton Essays in International Finance (1952).

3. See Richard N. Cooper, "Trade Policy and Foreign Policy," University of Michigan

Conference on U.S. Trade Policies in a Changing World Economy, March 28—29, 1985, p. 2. Cooper was Undersecretary of State for Economic Affairs in the Carter Administration.

4. See, for example, Robert Hudec, *The GATT Legal System and World Trade Diplomacy* (New York: Praeger, 1975) and John Jackson, *World Trade and the Law of the GATT* (New York: Bobbs Merrill, 1969).

5. According to Ernest Preeg, *Traders and Diplomats* (Washington: Brookings Institution, 1970), the Kennedy Round was economically and politically significant because "the inability to reach agreement would have encouraged opposition to a liberal trade policy and increased pressure for . . . higher tariffs . . . (and) the successful negotiation in the trade sector, played a vital role in relieving the general tension and misgivings of the period." pp. 260—61. John Evans, *The Kennedy Round in American Trade Policy: The Twilight of the GATT?* (Cambridge: Harvard University Press, 1971), p. 318 was more guarded, but agreed that "for nearly five years the negotiations provided a buffer against the pressures for protection of imports and allowed a truce in trade controversies." As his title suggests, he was less optimistic about the future.

6. OECD, *Policy Perspectives for International Trade and Economic Relations* (Paris: OECD, 1972). Report by the High-Level Group on Trade and Related Problems, Jean Rey, Chairman.

7. William B. Kelly, "Satisfactory Implementation of Most Tokyo Round Agreements," *GATT Focus*, #27 (January—February, 1984): p. 2. Kelly said the subsidy code is not working well and therefore has received the most public attention, primarily because of the ambiguous rules open to varying interpretation.

8. Gilbert Winham, *International Trade and the Tokyo Round Negotiations*, (forthcoming, Princeton University Press, 1986), agrees with Fred Bergsten and William Cline in their chapter "Conclusion and Policy Implications" in William Cline, ed., *Trade Policy for the 1980s* (Washington: Institute for International Economics, 1983), "the conventional wisdom is (that) the Tokyo Round made net contributions to an open trading system", (p. 768).

9. See Richard Cooper, *op. cit.*, p. 41.

10. For example, see Lydia Dunn, *In the Kingdom of the Blind* and Kenneth Durham, *Words are Not Enough*, both from the Trade Policy Research Centre, London (1983 and 1982, respectively) and the references therein. Both trace the undermining of GATT discipline back to precedents and procedures adopted in the early postwar period.

11. The Stockholm meeting also achieved a temporary breakthrough of sorts with regard to substance and structure. Before the meeting, the Koreans stated and the ASEAN nations signaled their willingness to participate in a new round. Ministers from Uruguay, Colombia, and the Philippines indicated their willingness to proceed to negotiations. More startling, the Brazilian Foreign Minister Setubal, against the advice of his bureaucrats, suggested that he was willing to allow preparation for negotiations to go ahead so long as two separate and parallel negotiations, under GATT auspices, were held for goods and services. Each negotiation could be held, but they would be "watertight" (i.e., no tradeoffs would be allowed between the negotiations). He noted that Brazil and other LDCs might not participate in the services negotiations. The end result would be a traditional negotiation on old issues and the development of a separate General Agreement for Services (GAS). With the exception of India, which remained adamantly opposed to inclusion of services on the agenda, there was strong support for this proposal from both industrial and developing countries.

Whether such a structure is feasible is less clear. Indeed, Brazil backed away from ("clarified") Setubal's formulation almost at once. Ultimately, developing countries which wish to negotiate about services may prefer to balance their concessions on services for industrial-country concessions in areas like textiles, footwear, agriculture, and steel. The Setubal formulation would seem to rule this out.

12. A round of negotiations also has a salutary educational effect. New cohorts of civil servants have to familiarize themselves with the rules of international trade.

13. The number of lawyers and interest groups in Washington dealing with trade issues has grown dramatically in recent years as trade law has become one of Washington's growth industries.

14. Charles Kindleberger has argued that the stability of the system depends in large part on the existence of a single country which, by virtue of its economic and political power, can act as a leader, both in absorbing shocks to the system and in cajoling and bullying the other members into cooperative efforts to resist protectionism. Charles Kindleberger, *The World in Depression, 1929–1939* (Berkeley, University of California Press, 1973). But also see extensions and critiques of Kindleberger's hegemonic leadership hypothesis: Robert O. Keohane, *After Hegemony* (Princeton: Princeton University Press, 1984) and Arthur Stein, "The Hegemon's Dilemma: Great Britain, the United States and the International Economic Order," in *International Organization* vol. 38 (1984), pp. 335–86.

15. Previous negotiations were completed during economic upturns. Although worldwide economic growth declined in the wake of the 1973 oil shock, the Tokyo Round was completed at a time when unemployment in the United States declined to under 6 percent for the first time since the mid-1970s recession.

16. OECD, *Economic Outlook* (Paris: OECD, June 1985).

17. See "Employment in Manufacturing," presented to the Joint Economic Committee by the Commissioner of the Bureau of Labor Statistics, June 7, 1985.

18. For a more complete discussion, see C. Michael Aho and Thomas O. Bayard, "The 1980s: Twilight of the Open Trading System?" in *The World Economy*, vol. 5, no. 4 (December 1982), pp. 379–406.

19. John Zysman, Stephen Cohen and Laura Tyson, *Creating Advantage: Adjusting to Change in a New World Economy*, Berkeley Roundtable in International Economics, forthcoming 1986. For a critical review of the literature on industrial policy, see Paul Krugman, "Strategic Sectors and International Competition," paper for University of Michigan Conference on U.S. Trade Policies in a Changing World Economy, March 28–29, 1985.

20. See Kenichi Ohmae, *Triad Power: The Coming Shape of Global Competition* (New York: Free Press, 1985).

21. Ironically, American multinationals which are spread most widely throughout the world might have the most to lose from liberalization.

Three

What Negotiations Could Accomplish

Two broad goals should characterize these talks: higher economic growth and greater international trade discipline. Higher growth will require trade liberalization, integrating the developing countries into the system and making progress on the new issues, such as services and high technology. Greater discipline will require strengthening and updating GATT, including both institutional reform and the resolution of long-standing issues such as safeguards and nontariff barriers. The issues reviewed here are familiar. They have all been under discussion and/or negotiation at least since the 1982 Ministerial Meeting and many for much longer.[1]

The distinction between growth and discipline is arbitrary; they go hand-in-hand. Greater discipline would reduce uncertainty and therefore spur investment and growth. Higher growth from greater market access and liberalization in services cannot be sustained unless international discipline is assured.

Higher Growth

All nations share a common interest in raising global economic growth. Certain measures will promote continued economic expansion or help provide new opportunities for growth in a new economic environment. To the extent that the aim of the new round is to spur economic growth, each nation has contributions to make and each will benefit in turn.

Increased Market Access

Industrial and developing countries seek greater access to each other's markets. The developing countries, particularly the upper-tier newly industrialized countries (NICs), OPEC countries, and, until recently, the high-debt Latin countries have been the most rapidly growing markets for industrial country exports. But most LDCs still have vast pools of underutilized resources with unemployment and underemployment rates running as high as 40 to 45 percent. If trade could be liberalized and these resources were to become employed, income and trade would expand rapidly.

Most trade between industrial and developing countries is complementary (along the lines of the traditional factor-endowment theory of comparative advantage). Industrial countries export capital goods and import consumer (labor-intensive) goods. For example, the share of U.S. exports of capital goods going to the developing countries rose from 30 percent in 1970 to 42 percent in 1980. In the same decade, the share of U.S. imports of consumer goods from developing countries rose from 25 to 50 percent.[2]

Integrating the developing countries into the GATT, with all the rights and responsibilities that this entails, could provide the greatest single boost to world growth. Employment of the surplus labor in LDCs would increase output and growth in much the same way as surplus labor was absorbed after World War II. The largest contribution to growth in the postwar period resulted from the shift of resources from less productive to more productive sectors. Similarly, today a shift from consumer-goods to capital-goods production in industrial countries (along with less reliance on protection in capital-goods sectors in developing countries) could pay growth dividends. At the same time, open markets would encourage all countries to specialize in areas in which they enjoy advantages and not try to produce every possible good and service.

If negotiations led to reciprocal bargaining which extended LDC access to all industrial countries, both sides would benefit and the world economy would receive the growth stimulus it so badly needs. Unfortunately, the industrial countries have many sticks but few carrots to encourage the developing countries to negotiate. There is some room for tariff cuts where tariff structures are escalated on processed products. However, the adjustment problems in industrial countries are most pronounced, and the political power is greatest in the labor-intensive sectors in which the LDCs are most competitive. It is in these sectors in which existing measures, tariff and nontariff barriers and the "voluntary" restraint agreements, are the most restrictive.[3]

Industrial-country leaders, to protect their political flanks, talk about excluding the key areas the LDCs are most interested in from the trade talks. This is a perfectly sensible bargaining position, but in the absence of potential liberalization in those sectors, negotiations with the LDCs may not get off the ground. Therefore, even while protesting that they will not concede an inch, the industrial countries must ultimately put these sectors onto the table. This will be necessary to get the LDCs to the table. By the time agreements must be reached, changed world-wide situations may allow for meaningful progress on LDC issues. At this stage, nothing needs to be given away except the willingness to talk.

Adjustment problems for industrial-country workers cannot be minimized because they are a potent political force and the burden of adjustment falls unevenly. Workers in more traditional, import-competing industries like textiles and apparel are on average less skilled, less educated, lower paid, older, and more likely to be female or members of minority groups. They are also the least occupationally mobile. Thus, workers who bear the brunt of the adjustment burden because of increased imports are least able to afford it. This contrasts sharply with the skilled and better educated workers needed in higher-technology export industries which are expanding because of increased interdependence. Trade does create new jobs—probably more than it destroys—but they are entirely different jobs, requiring entirely different skills.[4]

Achieving higher growth through trade talks depends critically on how labor market adjustment issues are handled. They must be addressed soon because competition from the developing countries will only increase over time. Today's children are tomorrow's workers, and population developments are reshaping the world labor force and the patterns of demand which will last well into the next century. Out of every 100 people added to the world's population in the next twenty years, 95 will be born in the developing world and only about 5 in the industrial countries. The implications for trade are immense. Competitive pressures on world markets will increase as the developing countries' need for new jobs and incomes climbs rapidly. At the same time, the enormous investment needs and consumer demand in the developing countries could make them the world's most dynamic markets in the years ahead.

What commitments would the LDCs be willing to make in new negotiations? What responsibility will they accept to promote increased world economic growth? Many LDCs retain high levels of protection in many capital-intensive and high-technology industries. These barriers could be phased out over time, particularly if the LDCs became convinced that they are counterproductive.

Developing countries might also accept greater reliance on market forces in allocating domestic resources. A contentious dispute is bound to center on how any new initiatives will affect the "special and differential" treatment which the LDCs now enjoy. Some of the more advanced developing countries will probably be asked to agree to a time or target schedule for graduation, at least on a sector-by-sector basis. We have more to say about special and differential treatment and graduation in Chapter 6.

Exceptional Sectors

Developing countries argue that the current trading regime is biased against them. The sectors in which they have comparative advantage according to the traditional factor endowment theory of trade—land and labor-intensive products—are the most protected. Special regimes govern trade in agriculture, textiles and apparel, and steel.

Agriculture has been an exception in GATT since the U.S. waiver for its domestic agricultural programs was granted in 1955.[5] The European Community (EC) subsequently protected its agricultural sector with an ingenious device of dubious legality in GATT terms. Agriculture is the best example of domestic economic policies which have significant international effects. The basic problem is that domestic price supports set prices higher than world prices; this requires import restrictions to protect domestic markets and encourages overproduction and surpluses, which lead to export subsidies. Trade liberalization and such domestic farm policies are inconsistent. The United States uses a variety of measures to support prices or subsidize farmers, together with an assortment of trade restrictions. The EC, through its Common Agricultural Policy (CAP), sets a domestic price level and uses a variable levy which fills the difference between the domestic price and the world price. Import restrictions distort trade but they are not the fundamental problem; domestic support programs are. The basic issue is whether countries are prepared to negotiate domestic agricultural prices and programs.

Complicating matters, as surpluses mount, countries look for third markets in which to sell. The lack of a stringent agreement curbing export subsidies in agriculture has led to the establishment of export subsidy programs in both the Community and the United States, and now the world is in danger of getting into an export subsidy war to dump the excess production. This is tragic and absurd. It is tragic because at the same time we have mountains of surplus butter and seas of excess grain, millions of people are starving.[6] It is absurd because agricultural programs are already costing governments billions of dollars annually. Three-quarters of the EC budget is devoted to financing the Common Agricultural Policy. In the United States, the budgetary outlays for agriculture have sky-rocketed in the last four years, going from $4 billion in 1980 to almost $20 billion in 1984, with additional off-budget costs of $10—12 billion. Uncounted billions are also lost due to the distortions caused throughout both economies because of the regulated prices.

Although they are the two largest producers, the United States and the EC are not the only ones with agricultural restrictions and distortions. Japan maintains high barriers to protect rural interests. Many developing countries have agricultural programs which distort trade. As if things were not bad enough, problems in agriculture could mushroom if the new biotechnologies have their expected impact in increasing yields and productivity. Together with the new production coming from countries like China and Brazil, these technologies will result in even larger surpluses, which in turn will put more pressure on budgets as support payments mount.

In an attempt to increase discipline, a Committee on Trade in Agricultural Products was established in GATT after the 1982 Ministerial Meeting. Together with the Agriculture Committee at the OECD, it is currently working to quantify the extent of agricultural subsidies. Given budgetary pressures in the EC and the United States, the hope is that each will be forced to cut back agricultural supports. Each could then claim credit in negotiations. The question is, who is going to move first?

Another set of problems arises because the rules for agriculture are not in conformity with those for trade in industrial products. The subsidy code treats agriculture differently by not prohibiting export subsidies for primary products as long as the subsidies are not used to acquire more than a "fair and equitable share of the market." But what is a primary product? Does it include products largely derived from primary products (wheat flour, pasta)? Market shares to assess fair and equitable treatment are based upon a representative three-year period. What is a representative period? Dispute-settlement panels have foundered on the lack of precision in the rules and the definitions. Much of the criticism of the subsidy code and the dispute-settlement process in GATT stems from this differential treatment of agriculture export subsidies.

Managed trade in *textiles* began in 1961 with the completion of the Short-Term Arrangement for trade in cotton goods. The arrangement was expanded and extended as the Long-Term Arrangement in 1962. Subsequently, woolens and man-made fibres were restricted as well. The present regime was legitimized with the signing of the Multifibre Arrangement (MFA) in 1974, renegotiated in 1977 and 1981, and is due to expire in the summer of 1986. Today the MFA covers the trade of 50 countries in over 3,000 separate products. Quotas are negotiated bilaterally between the importing country and the supplier.

What began as a temporary program to manage trade has turned into permanent protection. As long as it is perceived to be permanent, there will continue to be an incentive for resources to be diverted into the sector. Since the MFA is due to be renegotiated by the summer of 1986, there is some discussion that the agreement should be rolled over and included in the new round. This could allow tradeoffs to be made, say, expanded textile quotas in return for greater market discipline in LDCs. Tariffs are also high in these industries. An alternative method for liberalizing would be to remove portions of the textile and apparel industries from the MFA, leaving the tariffs in place. This would subject those parts of textiles and apparel to greater market discipline while still allowing them access to normal safeguard rules.[7]

Despite political pressure from affected industries in industrial countries, the phase-out over time of the quotas may be an essential element of the final negotiating package. The need for adjustment in the United States is illustrated by the fact that the textile industry, the most highly protected sector in the U.S. economy, also spends relatively little for research and development. The opportunity for adjustment is illustrated by the successful examples of Germany, Italy, and Britain. Germany, after allowing for adjustment in its textile industry, is now a leading exporter. Italy and Britain show improving export trends. Liberalization in the United States may be politically difficult, but it is not impossible. And, more open markets in textiles would give the LDCs a reason to participate in good faith in the coming trade talks.

The world economy also seems to be drifting into a regime of managed trade in *steel*. The European Community has been undertaking a substantial industrial restructuring in steel, supported by various forms of national government assistance and coordinated at the Community level. The United States has recently completed bilateral quota negotiations with over a dozen countries restricting trade in steel production. The net effect has been virtually to cartel-ize the world steel industry.

Almost everyone likes bilateral quotas and has a vested interest in their continuation. Once in place, they are difficult to remove. Domestic producers know how much will be imported. Foreign pro-ducers get high profits. Government bureaucrats have more to negotiate. The only opposition comes from economists, consumers, and potential new suppliers, and they are not an effective counter-vailing force.

This raises a fundamental question of whether more progress would be made in dealing with the difficult adjustment problems of basic industries like steel if new procedures or rules were estab-lished for discussing such issues within the GATT. The history of the MFA may be a poor model for multilateral discussions in exceptional sectors. But, is there an alternative? Multilateral discussions of these problems would be better than bilateral ones because smaller trad-ing nations and newcomers have little leverage in bilateral talks.

Services

Service industries such as banking, insurance, telecommunica-tions, data processing, construction and transportation are growing increasingly important in the world economy. Nonetheless, trade in services is hampered by a wide variety of government measures that restrict or discriminate against imported services. The United States, Canada, and Japan advocate that the next round attempt to develop new rules, principles and procedures to manage trade in services. In March 1985, the European Community officially added its support.

The push for rules to govern trade in services is consistent with the long-term restructuring within countries and in the world econ-omy as a whole. Services also are increasing as inputs into the pro-duction of goods. A world information economy is emerging which is allowing services to be traded which never could be traded before (e.g., consulting, legal, data processing, design services). In essence, services, particularly financial and telecommunication services, are the infrastructure on which future growth will depend. Unless countries extend the trading system to cover services and other related items such as international flows of information, pro-tection with regard to services could significantly hamper future trade in goods and services. Growth would suffer.[8]

Services account for a growing percentage of jobs and GNP in all industrial countries. In 1984 about 68 percent of GNP and over 73 percent of U.S. employment (57 percent if government is excluded) came from services. Other industrial countries lag only a little behind the United States. In addition, most of the new jobs being created in the industrial countries are service jobs. At a time when more jobs are needed to absorb new labor force entrants and layoffs in the traditional goods sectors, creation of service jobs is important as a component of long-term structural adjustment policy.[9] Proponents of services claim that this reason alone justifies inclusion of services in a new round. Finally, while conceding that services may not be in crisis today, proponents fear that if action on services is postponed until the 1990s, protectionism against trade in services will increase and all countries will pay the cost. If fast-changing service sectors are not dealt with now, years will be lost, which will hurt future prospects for liberalization.

However, critics in many countries have reservations about the advisability of tackling these complex and fluid sectors. The issues go beyond traditional commercial considerations and include questions of culture, privacy and national security. The sectors are heterogeneous and the restrictions are often not comparable. Services are usually more regulated by governments than goods and are often provided by government-owned or government-controlled monopolies. Some services, like insurance, are regulated at the state level in the United States or at the regional level in other countries. Trade ministers in many countries do not have the competence or authority to negotiate in service industries because other agencies regulate these sectors. For example, few expect much progress on banking because finance ministries, including the U.S Treasury Department, have no intention of allowing trade ministers to discuss issues so closely related to monetary and exchange-rate policy. To compound the problems, modern technology is rapidly transforming many of these sectors and it is difficult to separate the trade and investment aspects of services transactions.

With so many complicating factors, how would negotiations on services proceed? The vague work program on services agreed to at the 1982 GATT Ministerial Meeting called for individual countries to conduct national studies, but no multilateral review was specified. Although a number of studies of differing thoroughness were submitted and discussed, progress between 1983 and 1985 proceeded slowly. The LDCs fought to deny GATT competence for services. Preparations for substantive negotiations on services are moving slowly. But now that all key industrial countries are on record favoring the inclusion of services on the agenda, work will go forward with or without the participation of the LDCs. To start, the Quadrilateral partners will seek an umbrella framework agreement and a standstill on new restrictions. Once that work is under way, they are likely to begin to focus on specific sectors such as telecommunications and insurance.[10]

Government Support in High-Technology Industries

The debate over issues involving high-technology, research-intensive industries such as semiconductors and telecommunications equipment revolves around whether, how, and to what extent countries should promote and protect dynamic sectors within their national economies. New industries which exhibit above-average productivity growth are often granted special status in national industrial development plans. In 1981, in an effort to push tariffs on semiconductors to zero, representatives of the U.S. electronics industry urged that high-technology product sectors should be treated separately. Subsequently, the high-technology area became the center of debate over government procurement policies in the telecommunications equipment sector and over Japanese targeting policies. The United States pushed for work on high technology at the 1982 GATT Ministerial Meeting, but did not convince other countries that high-technology industries should be handled any differently from other industries. The initiative was so poorly defined that LDC representatives asked how high-technology discussions could be related to transfer of technology, which is a legitimate question but not what the United States had in mind.

Meanwhile, confusion reigns on what practices are legitimate to use in the development of an industrial sector. Some practices are partially covered by the Tokyo Round NTB codes for standards, government procurement, and subsidies. Others, however, are not. The balkiness of the dispute-settlement processes in GATT means that decisions on questionable practices come slowly, if at all, and with rapid technological change, that is likely to be too late. The United States would like to extend the code coverage to include more products under the government procurement code and more practices under the standards code. It would also like to develop rules related to R&D subsidies and government-sponsored research, which may create long-lasting competitive advantage for firms and are difficult to countervail against.

The basis for the argument is that in this rapidly changing world in which technological advance can quickly alter the conditions of competition, government commitment and protection can create competitive advantages for firms. Initially, these firms may be protected behind restrictive barriers until they can achieve dynamic economies of scale through learning by doing. Access to a relatively open foreign market also helps to achieve these scale economies more quickly. Once the advantage is established, the firm can successfully penetrate foreign markets. But since the firm is often no longer receiving government support or subsidy, countervailing duties are not appropriate.

What should the role of the government be in supporting research, development and innovation? To the extent that these are hampered by elements of market imperfections (e.g., scale economies, R&D externalities, etc.) there is a legitimate role for the government. But when several governments are supporting large-scale efforts in the same sectors, their policies are going to clash internationally. Even small promotion efforts can create friction because there is no multilateral agreement on which policies are acceptable. As the distinction between international and domestic economic policies continues to blur, is it possible to judge what is acceptable internationally and what is not? The United States accuses Japan of industrial targeting largely on the basis of the long-term visions put out by the Ministry of International Trade and Industry (MITI). But, what about U.S. defense expenditures or its agricultural service?[11]

High-technology policies related to the promotion of national security, the regulation of technology transfer, extra-territoriality, and export controls often infringe on national prerogatives and sovereignty and make codification of additional rules difficult. Unless the United States defines its objectives clearly and admits that security-related programs such as the Strategic Defense Initiative are a high-technology industrial policy, little will happen in trade talks in this area.

Greater Discipline

The policy dilemma in new negotiations is not one of free trade versus protectionism. It is a question of rules and discipline, of who obeys and who does not, and of what is fair and what is not. Unless international discipline improves, policy makers will find it impossible to convince citizens and firms that they should obey the rules when they believe that no one else is playing by them. Without discipline, businesses cannot plan effectively on a global basis. But discipline requires greater cooperation, which is lacking today. And it requires a good dose of institutional updating.

Institutional Reform

A major aim of the negotiations should be the enhancement and updating of GATT. Reform is needed to improve trade relations, to re-establish GATT's prestige, and to get the GATT system ready to respond to the changing world economy.

If they were up-to-date and widely accepted, GATT rules and procedures could allow government leaders to do what they know is in the national interest even in the face of pressure to help narrower, special interests. But discipline is lacking and exceptions are the rule, so that GATT cannot be leaned on to resist taking restrictive actions. Today, more than 90 percent of all import-safeguard actions, on a value basis, are handled outside of GATT. To the extent possible, difficult problems which are now handled outside of GATT must be accommodated within the system. Otherwise the credibility of the system will continue to erode. Several reforms are critical.[12]

The dispute-settlement process in GATT is inadequate; some cases have languished for years. Improved procedures are essential in a world in which technology can change the shape of competition almost overnight. Dispute-settlement procedures need to be more uniform and timely, and disputants must be convinced that they should abide by decisions.

One method for checking the spread of trade restrictions is to assure that they are visible and held up to the scrutiny of public opinion, both domestically and internationally. It is often forgotten that the distributional consequences of trade restrictions are felt internally, not among nations. Member countries need to find a way to increase public awareness of the cost of trade restrictions and to engage the stakeholders who have an interest in open trade. Exporters, retailers, consumers and banks among others have to mobilize to express their positions on trade policy because they stand to lose if the discussion is one-sided, dominated by import-competing interests. Greater awareness of the domestic conflicts of interest could result in fewer unilateral actions and thereby enhance the credibility of the trading system.

Trade restrictions and violations should also be made more transparent internationally. The GATT Secretariat does not have sufficient authority to publicize trade restrictions and violations of GATT commitments. In international trade, just as in traffic, following accepted rules enhances freedom of action and reduces uncertainty. But with traffic, the police enforce the rules to serve the general interest. For trade, no enforcement authority can arrest violators to serve the general interest. Stiff, sure, swift sanctions are not available to deter potential offenders. There is no impartial third party to take the initiative in responding to emerging trade problems. Countries with legitimate complaints of infractions of GATT rules may not file them, because the other country is stronger or because they are bought off—sometimes at the expense of some third country. Although this may be rational for a country, the action damages the system. Today, no one represents the system. The system needs defending.

Short of formal dispute-settlement procedures, other procedural changes would improve trade relations. In the absence of agreement among the contracting parties on improvements in substantive rules, reform of procedural rules could help minimize trade conflicts. Frequently, an agreement to keep certain kinds of situations under surveillance is the most that can be achieved.

Multilateral surveillance needs to be upgraded so that developments can be monitored and policy changes can be recommended on a more timely basis. As it now stands, circumventions of GATT rules are not discussed in a systematic manner. Countries are not held accountable for their trade practices. For those trade issues not adequately covered by the rules, complaints procedures together with mediation and conciliation services would also help to resolve disputes or grievances as they arise. Establishment of procedures for lodging complaints would help to determine which practices are fair and which are not so that a body of precedents could be developed over time.

The increased pluralism in the world economy has created decision-making problems for GATT and threatens to politicize GATT, turning it into another forum for airing North-South issues. The consensus decision-making in GATT could prove its undoing unless a new streamlined decision process can be agreed upon. The creation of an ongoing consultative process/arena (or even stronger, an executive committee or trade policy board) would help countries reach consensus on emerging problems. Ministerial meetings are held too infrequently, and so trade problems do not receive enough attention by top-level trade officials. If Ministers gathered more often, affected third-party interests could be addressed more easily and progress might be made on some politically sensitive bilateral issues.

As a growing force in international trade, the developing countries need to be brought into the bargaining process of GATT. They are now accorded special and differential treatment through preferences and easier access to exceptions and are not required to make reciprocal concessions in negotiations. In short, they are different and the industrial countries treat them differently. Because they are marginal to the process, they have little leverage to change aspects of the system which discriminate against them. However, if they are willing to accept greater responsibilities and participate more fully in the bargaining process, they will acquire more rights and exercise more positive influence. For the system to work better, LDCs need to become first-class citizens.

Finally, GATT lacks a permanent negotiating committee which could respond to issues susceptible to negotiation between rounds. The review committees established under the nontariff barrier codes were to serve a similar purpose but they have yielded little. If ongoing multilateral negotiations were under way, this would also help to strengthen the resolve of politicians to resist supporting unilateral actions.

In sum, institutional changes are needed to ensure that trade issues are dealt with on an ongoing basis with procedures that could be applied as new issues emerge. If such changes could be agreed to in a new round, the system would become more flexible and a stronger Secretariat would have a better chance to further the general interest. The process could be self-reinforcing. Greater discipline and respect for GATT processes would strengthen the position of policy makers in rejecting requests for unilateral trade restrictions for international obligations and multilateral processes could be cited.

Safeguards and Adjustment in Basic Industries

Safeguards, governing emergency protection in import-sensitive industries, are the most important unfinished business left over from the Tokyo Round. Article XIX of the GATT was to provide an "escape clause" under which countries could, in certain well-defined circumstances, impose import restrictions on a nondiscriminatory basis. Article XIX permits countries to suspend an obligation or withdraw a concession if "as a result of unforeseen developments" imports cause or threaten to cause serious injury to domestic producers. There is a requirement for prior notification and consultation. Consultation can result in a modification of the action, payment of compensation by the imposing country, or a withdrawal of equivalent concessions by the affected country. Over the years, however, Article XIX has fallen into disuse and bilateral circumventions such as voluntary export restraints have expanded. One recent example of a safeguards case was the U.S. action on specialty steel in 1983 when the United States increased restrictions. Consultations were held in GATT without a resolution so the EC retaliated, extracting compensation through new restrictions against U.S. sports equipment, alarm systems, and some chemical products.

A workable safeguards code needs to provide a multilateral method for addressing difficult industrial problems that are now most often dealt with through bilateral circumventions. The problems are familiar. Should safeguard actions under a new code be applied only on a nondiscriminatory basis, or could limited selectivity with notification, consultation and surveillance be adopted? Selectivity would allow a country to impose trade barriers on a specific country or group of countries rather than imposing barriers on a MFN basis. The developing countries, in particular, are concerned about maintaining market access. They feel that the circumventions have been targeted against them in a discriminatory fashion. They prefer a new code to provide for only nondiscriminatory application of safeguards. They argue that application of a safeguard is not a punishment for an offending exporter but an admission that the industry is not competitive. Since nondiscrimination affects all suppliers, they have a common interest in early removal of the restrictions, and this concentrates the pressure for adjustment where it ought to be—on the protecting country and its noncompetitive industry. The European Community prefers selectivity.

The 1982 Ministerial Meeting sought to deal with safeguards but in the end only principles (transparency, coverage, gradual phase-outs and time limits) were agreed upon and additional negotiations were scheduled. Those negotiations have so far been stalemated.

Safeguards also raise the question of structural adjustment in response to changes in trade. More emphasis needs to be put on structural adjustment internationally, and the GATT is the logical place to hold multilateral discussions on structural adjustment. Any new code or understanding should explicitly link safeguards and adjustment.

Nontariff Barrier Codes

The subsidies, government procurement, and standards codes negotiated during the Tokyo Round need to be fully implemented, enforced and extended. To some degree, these codes were oversold to the legislatures and parliaments which ratified the agreements. Now, the limited coverage of these codes and their perceived lack of international discipline, particularly with regard to subsidies, is undermining the credibility of the system.

A thorough review of the codes' operation would help expose the deficiencies. Why have review committees not functioned as they were designed—as ongoing fora for discussion and resolution of issues? The codes were meant to begin, not to end, the process.

The subsidies code, for example, needs to be revamped to put industrial and agricultural products on the same clear standard. What constitutes a "fair and equitable share of the market" is subject to varying interpretations and renders implementation and enforcement of the subsidy code for agricultural products almost impossible.

Subsidies and to a lesser extent government procurement go to the heart of the fairness question, but it is difficult to measure the extent to which they distort trade. It is an empirical question how much subsidies imposed for domestic purposes distort trade and injure foreign countries. More difficult still is the extent to which subsidies for R&D or preferential government treatment may create a permanent advantage for an industry. Lacking a multilateral agreement on what practices are unfair, countries (especially the United States) are unilaterally defining unfairness and, when they consider it legitimate, impose countervailing duties. It may prove impossible to write new substantive rules, but new procedural rules should be adopted in order to improve discipline over subsidies.[13]

This raises a more general point. The world has changed since the GATT was formed. Developing substantive rules to cover new practices has lagged. Ironically, the success in reducing tariffs has exposed existing nontariff barriers and subsidies and led to the erection of new ones which are less transparent than tariffs. More analytical work needs to be done to determine the restrictiveness of existing NTBs and to develop the framework for negotiations because NTBs are less susceptible to reciprocal negotiations than tariffs.[14] The difficulties involved will require an ongoing process which provides for frequent consultation and exchange among negotiators from different countries.

Counterfeiting and Intellectual Property

The counterfeiting of trademarked commercial merchandise and the theft and duplication of intellectual property have become international problems which are spreading and increasing each year. The U.S. International Trade Commission estimates that $6 billion in trade entering the United States annually is counterfeit.

In 1979, the United States and the European Community reached agreement (ad referendum) on the text of a code to deter international trade in counterfeited trademarked merchandise. Over the next two years, the United States and European Community intensified efforts to broaden participation in the code. This effort resulted in multilateral discussions with a number of GATT countries, including Canada and Japan. The United States, the European Community, Canada and Japan reached agreement on a revised ad referendum text and agreed to have the text circulated by the GATT Secretariat. They also proposed that it be used as the basis for negotiating a code generally acceptable to all GATT members.

Although the draft agreement was accepted in principle by the four major players, the counterfeit code was shelved at the GATT Ministerial Meeting by instructing the Council to examine the issue further. Some developing countries opposed any mention of the issue at the Ministerial, arguing that it falls within the competence of the World Intellectual Property Organization (WIPO), not the GATT. The Ministerial requested that the Director-General hold consultations with the Director-General of WIPO to clarify the issue and determine the appropriateness of joint action, but thus far little progress has been made. Unless counterfeiting is addressed on an international level, individual countries probably will act unilaterally because political pressure is increasing for greater control over trade in counterfeit products.

Intellectual property is the new extension of the old problem of counterfeiting. Manufacturing firms seek substantive protection of their patent, trademark, and trade secret rights. Service firms are concerned with copyright protection for their software, publications, music, movies, broadcasts, and innovations that increasingly are "borrowed" without paying royalties or licensing fees. High-level U.S. officials have begun pressuring Hong Kong, Singapore, Taiwan, Korea and other countries where such practices are common to clamp down on intellectual property offenders. U.S. officials suggest that without stronger protection for foreign intellectual property, potential new investors might be more reluctant to establish themselves and transfer their knowledge and technology. Already, to the extent that reverse engineering is difficult, large firms are keeping new breakthroughs as trade secrets rather than copyrighting or patenting them.[15] This hampers the theft of intellectual property, but also slows the diffusion of new knowledge to those who might benefit from it.

Most existing agreements involving intellectual property protection are administered under WIPO. They build on the principle of national treatment and aim to harmonize divergent national laws. Statutes vary significantly from country to country; enforcement is usually weak or nonexistent. Provisions for the settlement of international disputes are lacking. Progress is needed to extend intellectual property rights internationally, to work for the enforcement of these rights, to provide consultation and dispute settlement mechanisms, and to assure that countervailing moves can be taken against countries which ignore intellectual property rights.

Trade-distorting Investment Practices

The use of local content rules and export performance requirements, which distort trade, has spread in recent years. The Mexican auto decree is the classic example of an investment policy which distorts trade, but even industrial countries, including the United States, have flirted with the idea of local-content rules. According to the U.S. Trade Representative's Office, some 30 countries now employ some form of investment requirements.[16] Unless international agreement is reached about what is acceptable behavior with respect to the use of these measures, trade conflicts arising from their use will multiply. As constituted at present, the GATT does not cover investment matters generally, but some existing agreements might be used to address trade-distorting investment practices.[17] Investment requirements not linked to trade covering the remission of profits, employment of residents, or ownership fall outside of the GATT. Investment requirements which discriminate against imports may conflict with GATT. Export requirements could be inconsistent with GATT if they are linked to subsidies.

The GATT contracting parties need to decide if a special effort is required to address these practices or if they could be handled under existing agreements like the subsidy code. Using existing rules and codes might be preferable, because discussions of codes of conduct for multinational corporations have bogged down at the United Nations and the OECD. The problems with using existing rules or codes are that LDCs could invoke "special and differential" treatment to get around the rules and only a handful of LDCs have subscribed to the subsidy code.

***

Multilateral trade negotiations have two stages. First, countries get things going and point discussions in certain directions. Details and understandings are worked out during extended talks. Second, as deadlines approach and fear of failure mounts, political leaders at the highest levels intervene to clinch bargains that their subordinates do not have the clout to conclude. This happened in the Kennedy and the Tokyo Rounds and will, if all goes well, happen again in the coming round.

Analysts prognosticating the outcome of a new round, at least at this stage, can speculate on the ultimate outcome as they choose. The primary focus, however, needs to be on the first level. How do we get into negotiations? How do we orient them and push them off in the right direction? It is at least as important to understand the context and the constraints that national politics and economics put on the launching of the negotiations as it is to predict how they will influence their outcome. By the time final agreements are reached and ratified in the world capitals, current macroeconomic conditions, the value of the dollar, the U.S. budget deficit, the debt situation, the energy situation, the leaders of most of the participating countries, and the competitive structure of the world economy all will have changed.

We turn now to a discussion of the domestic constraints in the countries which will be major players in the negotiations. An awareness of these constraints is essential, in part so that governments do not promise more than they can deliver, and also in part because other policy initiatives could be designed to relax or remove the constraints. After the discussion of domestic constraints facing the major players, we shall present a global bargain in Chapter 8 from which all countries might gain.

Notes

1. Detailed examinations of these issues are available in several sources. For a U.S. business perspective, see the Statement of the United States Council for International Business, "A New Round of Multilateral Trade Negotiations: Recommended U.S.

Business Objectives," April 18, 1985. Gary Clyde Hufbauer and Jeffrey Schott, *Trading for Growth: The Next Round of Trade Negotiations* (Washington: Institute for International Economics, September 1985) also have an issue focus along with a thumbnail sketch of a proposed solution in each issue area. Most analyses distinguish between old and new issues; we prefer to distinguish between measures that are needed to ensure continued growth in the world economy and those which are necessary to provide a discipline so that the trading system does not deteriorate further.

2. For a description of the longer-term trends in the commodity composition of U.S. trade, see William Branson, "Trends in United States International Trade and Investment since World War II," in Martin Feldstein, ed., *The American Economy in Transition* (Chicago: University of Chicago Press, 1980).

3. For a discussion of the politics of protection, see Robert Baldwin, "U.S. Trade Policy Since World War II," in Robert Baldwin and Anne O. Krueger, eds., *The Structure and Evolution of Recent U.S. Trade Policy* (Chicago: University of Chicago Press, 1984) and the references therein.

4. See C. Michael Aho and James A. Orr, "The Growth of Trade-Sensitive Employment", *Monthly Labor Review*, vol. 104, no. 2 (February 1981), pp. 29—35.

5. Agriculture is a long-standing problem which has not changed much over the years. For a good summary of the issues and why liberalization is so difficult, see Chapter 8 "Agriculture: Structure or Change?" in William Diebold, *The United States and the Industrial World*, (New York: Praeger for the Council on Foreign Relations, 1972). As Diebold says in commenting upon two books on agriculture written in 1949 and 1950, "The two books could have been written five years earlier or later and said much the same thing. A good bit of it is still true today (1972)." The same could be said in 1985.

6. See Barbara Insel, "A World Awash in Grain," in *Foreign Affairs*, vol. 63 no. 4 (Spring 1985), pp. 892—911.

7. See GATT, *Textiles and Clothing in the World Economy* (Geneva: GATT, 1984) for a detailed background of the textile industry.

8. Geza Feketekuty and Jonathan Aronson, "Meeting the Challenges of the World Information Economy," *The World Economy*, vol. 7, no. 1 (March 1984), pp. 63—86; Jonathan Aronson and Peter F. Cowhey, *Trade In Services: A Case for Open Markets* (Washington: American Enterprise Institute, 1984); and Harald Malmgren, "Negotiating International Rules for Trade in Services," in *The World Economy*, vol. 8, no. 1 (March 1985), pp. 11—26.

9. See "Services: The New Economy," special supplement, *Fortune*, June 10, 1985, pp. 166—202.

10. See statements by the United States and the EC at the Quadrilateral Meeting of Trade Ministers at Sioux St. Marie, Canada, July 11—14, 1985.

11. For a summary comparison of industrial policies in the United States, Japan, France, West Germany and Great Britain, see Richard Nelson, *High-Technology Policies: A 5-Nation Comparison* (Washington: American Enterprise Institute, 1984). For an earlier analysis of the problems of defining industrial policies and the complications they create for the trading system, see William Diebold, *Industrial Policy as an International Issue* (New York: McGraw Hill, 1980).

12. For a more detailed discussion of the system's inadequacies and proposals for reform, see Miriam Camps and William Diebold, *The New Multilateralism* (New York: Council on Foreign Relations, 1983).

13. For an extended treatment, see Gary Clyde Hufbauer and Joanna Shelton-Erb, *Subsidies in International Trade* (Washington: Institute for International Economics, 1984).

14. One method would be to convert existing NTBs to tariffs so that the restrictions allow market forces to operate and then seek to reduce the tariffs over time. This raises difficult compensation problems, but it would promote transparency and allocation by market forces.

15. See Dennis Unkovic, *The Trade Secrets Handbook: Strategies and Techniques for Safeguarding Corporate Information* (Englewood: Prentice Hall, Inc., 1985).

16. For an analysis of the issues, see Harvey Bale, "Trade Policy Aspects of International Direct Investment Policies," in Robert Baldwin, ed., *Recent Issues and Initiatives in U.S. Trade Policy*, NBER Conference Report, 1983.

17. Article 12 of the ITO Charter, according to which members of the ITO would have agreed "to provide reasonable opportunities for investments acceptable to them and adequate security for existing and future investments," reflected so little agreement that it proved unacceptable to U.S. business and was not taken over into GATT.

Part II
National Goals and Constraints

Four

The United States

The United States has championed every postwar multilateral trade round. The Reagan Administration seeks new trade negotiations to strengthen and extend the trading system by addressing issues such as services, high-technology products, intellectual property, dispute settlement, safeguards and agriculture where it feels the United States has something to gain. It also hopes new trade negotiations will halt further disintegration of the trading system and distract attention from the growing trade imbalance. They have bought the bicycle theory, lock, stock and barrel.

Global recession, the debt problem, and the hesitation of some and opposition of other major trading nations prevented the Reagan Administration from getting agreement to launch a new round at the 1982 Ministerial Meeting. In 1985, the timing is better. The U.S. government has finally won support from the major industrial countries to launch new trade negotiations, and, if GATT concurs, they could begin by mid-1986. That was the easy part. Now, the Administration, in consultation with Congress and the private sector, must decide what and how to negotiate, in light of what other countries want as concessions. Then it will have to develop and sustain the domestic consensus necessary to complete a successful negotiation.

What difficult issues will the United States be willing to discuss? That battle remains to be fought in the domestic political arena, and the answer will determine how ambitious the negotiations will be. Because of its Constitutional authority, Congress will play a critical role. But Congress is awash in over 300 protectionist bills. It is focused on trade restriction and correcting the mounting trade deficit rather than on trade liberalization.

The strong dollar has helped to create a U.S. trade deficit which topped $123 billion in 1984 and could reach $150 billion in 1985. In economic terms, trade deficits are not in and of themselves a problem, but politically trade deficits act like a lightning rod—more so, when exports are stagnant. U.S. exports in 1984 were less than in

1980, while U.S. imports exceeded their 1980 levels by 60 percent (75 percent in manufacturing). Legislators cannot count on hearing about the virtues of open trade from exporters when their sales overseas are suffering.

Successful trade negotiations would increase world-wide growth and would help restore confidence in the trading system; failure would further undermine the system. Which will it be? That will depend on the strength of the Administration's commitment to trade liberalization and its willingness and political ability to take some difficult domestic steps at a time when labor, business, and the public are growing more protectionist.[1] Six main constraints handicap U.S. negotiators as they enter new negotiations.

Constraint: The Relative Decline of U.S. Economic Power

Over the past two decades, the competitive position of the United States in world markets and in the domestic market has eroded. The increased competition facing U.S. producers is largely the result of changing world resource supplies and technological capabilities. Higher rates of growth in investment, expanded foreign research activity, and, some say, industrial targeting overseas have led to a relative decline in U.S. trade performance and a narrowing of the range of products in which the United States enjoys a competitive advantage.[2] These factors are the secular influences causing a deterioration in the U.S. competitive position. Other factors often cited include poor management, poor product quality, over-priced labor, a deterioration in the work ethic, over-much emphasis on short-term payoffs, and competitiveness not being a policy priority.

To some degree the relative U.S. decline was predictable. The United States emerged from World War II with its industrial base intact, assuring its initial pre-eminence. As other countries rebuilt and moved forward, U.S. pre-eminence slipped. The United States grew less dominant in international trade and the world economy, even as international trade became more important to the United States. Since 1960, trade (exports plus imports), as a percentage of U.S. GNP, more than doubled from 8 percent to over 20 percent in 1985. The erosion of U.S. economic dominance diminished its ability to dictate the outcome of international negotiations.

As trade grew more important to the United States, the sensitivity of the economy to changes in trade heightened and the domestic consensus for trade liberalization weakened. Imports are having significant effects on the industrial structure of the U.S. economy. The Department of Commerce estimates that today over 70 percent of U.S. manufacturing faces import competition. At the same time, the exporters' stake in open international markets has expanded. The number of manufacturing jobs directly and indirectly related to manufactured exports rose from one in fourteen in 1964 to one in seven by 1980. Exports as a percentage of final sales more than doubled during the 1970s. However, the significant appreciation of the dollar since 1980 means that, at least temporarily, the export sectors have less of a stake in trade liberalization.

Trade policy always has been more entwined with domestic politics than international monetary or exchange-rate policies.[3] Recently, however, the increased sensitivity of the U.S. economy to changes in the international economy has heightened American public awareness of the effect of trade policy on the economy. Public policy is increasingly being asked to choose between the general interest and the special interests of workers and industries being hurt by international competition.

Constraint: Building Domestic Consensus

Among traditional advocates of open markets in the business community, there is no groundswell of support for new negotiations. The strongest supporters come from sectors interested in one or more of the new issues; they see potential gains. Others are not so sure.[4]

The coalition strongly supporting a new round of negotiations is comprised mostly of the service industries, with high-technology interests, parts of agriculture, and the anticounterfeiting and intellectual property rights groups playing some role. The more traditional supporters, major exporters in the business community, are unenthusiastic because their competitive position has deteriorated so substantially with the appreciation of the dollar. By most estimates, the dollar in early 1985 was overvalued by 25 to 40 percent, which is equivalent to a tax on domestic producers or a subsidy to foreign producers of that amount. To listen to many business representatives talk about the need for simultaneous action on the currency front, one would think their words were drafted by the French government.

To begin developing the domestic consensus, in early 1985 U.S. Trade Representative Brock asked Edmund Pratt, the chief executive

officer of Pfizer, Inc., and Chairman of the Advisory Committee on
Trade Negotiations (ACTN), to conduct a major survey of private
sector views on the new round. Pratt mobilized the private sector
advisory committees and sought their input on the desirability of a
new round. (The private sector advisory committee structure was
established by the Trade Act of 1974 to receive private sector input on
the conduct of negotiations in the Tokyo Round. The advisory committee structure was extended in slightly modified form by the Trade
Agreements Act of 1979 which implemented the Tokyo Round
agreements. Today, in addition to the overall ACTN, there are eight
policy advisory committees and some three dozen technical and
sectoral advisory committees which meet regularly. Input from
these groups, although not legally binding, is essential for the USTR
to obtain because the U.S. Congress wants it.)

The report that emerged gave qualified support for new negotiations, but sent a strong call for action on exchange rates. "New multilateral negotiations alone are incapable of dealing with the overall
U.S. trade crisis. . . . The great majority of groups surveyed strongly
recommend that negotiations on exchange rates and financial issues
take place simultaneously with a new round of trade negotiations."[5]
Not only is business support lukewarm, but some sectors have met
to organize their outright opposition to a new round.

Constraint: Gaining Congressional Backing

Trade policy depends critically upon the relations between the President and Congress. The Constitution authorizes the Congress to
"lay and collect duties" and "to regulate foreign commerce". The
role of the President derives from a delegation of authority from the
Congress.

Congress will have to vote twice on the coming negotiations:
once to delegate the continuing authority to negotiate and again to
implement the agreement. Past experience suggests that a strong
domestic consensus, usually led by business interests, is needed to
steer a negotiation through Congress successfully. To date, the U.S.
trade deficit and the high dollar have thwarted Administration
efforts to shore up the domestic consensus. Votes in 1985 sharply
critical of Japan suggest that Congress is in no mood for trade liberalization, certainly not unreciprocated liberalization. Key Congressional leaders are calling for action on exchange rates and U.S.
competitiveness before negotiations begin.

Negotiating authority will have to be renewed because the provisions which require speedy Congressional consideration (the fast-track procedures) expire on January 3, 1988.[6] Although technically the President can negotiate anything he wants, and negotiations could begin even without a new trade act, U.S. trading partners may be reluctant to negotiate unless the President has explicit authority. Other countries feel that they were double crossed in earlier negotiations when Congress imposed additional conditions or rejected agreements after months and years of tedious negotiation. The Congressional delegation of authority is needed for the Administration to be credible in the negotiations.

What will it take to convince Congress to go along? Congress is wary about rolling festering trade problems into the preparatory process, as happened in the early stages of the Tokyo Round. Industries and workers were told not to worry, that their grievances would be dealt with during the negotiations. Most were not. Will Congress accept these promises again and allow outstanding problems to be rolled into a negotiating process which will take years?

Many business and Congressional supporters of trade liberalization believe, along with Will Rogers, that the United States has never won a negotiation. They are angry because they feel that others take advantage of U.S. good intentions and give nothing in return. This time, Congress is not enthusiastic about negotiations. Senator John Danforth (R., Mo.), Chairman of the Finance Committee's International Trade Subcommittee, opposed granting negotiating authority until the dollar comes down and outstanding trade problems are resolved.[7] A Democratic task force on international trade, chaired by Texas Senator Lloyd Bentsen, opposed an early start of negotiations until action is taken on U.S. competitiveness problems and until a comprehensive trade strategy is developed.[8]

Congress also is wary because it feels it was oversold on the progress that was achieved during the Tokyo Round on the nontariff barrier codes, particularly in subsidies and government procurement. The subsidy code has been a disappointment. It has been likened to trying to put out a forest fire with a handkerchief. U.S. complaints on wheat flour and pasta have not been resolved by dispute-settlement panels because of the fuzziness of the rules (e.g., what constitutes "a fair and equitable share of the market" and unclear definitions of primary and processed products) and because panel decisions are not binding. In the year ending March 31, 1985, U.S. companies got only $130 million of the roughly $3

billion in procurement purchases made by Nippon Telegraph and
Telephone (NTT). A significant proportion of these sales consisted
of items such as paper stock, and no meaningful breakthrough in
the purchase of switching equipment is in sight. And this is a limited success! Telecommunications equipment is not covered under
the code in any country except Japan.

With these experiences in mind, Congress is reluctant to
endorse new agreements in which greater access or stronger discipline are not apparent. In Japan, for example, they want to see
increasing imports of sophisticated products and services. Congress has no more patience with procedural reforms. Congress
wants results. But, if the Administration overstates the likelihood of
progress and unrealistic expectations are not met, the dissolution of
the system could follow in the wake of failed negotiations.

Complicating matters, the negotiation will be different from
those of the past because less time will be spent upon reciprocal
tariff-cutting, which policy makers could follow and understand.
The negotiations will have to focus more on NTBs and on an updating of GATT by improving or extending the rules of the game. Safeguards, dispute settlement, subsidies, and institutional reforms will
all require rule changes or refinements. Key issues will revolve
around efforts to make barriers transparent and to deal with invisi-
bles. To its credit, the Administration is pushing for stronger rules
and an updating of GATT. But little reciprocity is involved in these
issues.

The virtual elimination of tariffs as a barrier to trade also raises
touchy questions about committee jurisdiction in Congress. In the
House, the Energy and Commerce Committee has authority over
services and is trying to expand its authority to cover nontariff barriers. It was Energy and Commerce which reported out the local content bill in 1983 for automobiles. Trade policy is becoming an
entrepreneurial activity for staff on rival committees, and this
threatens the authority of the traditional trade committees, Finance
and Ways and Means. The required legislation may be harder to
achieve than in the past.

Can Congress be convinced to go along with an agreement
which offers only new or better rules? Imagine members of Congress going back to their districts and telling their constituents, "I've
gotten a better rule for you." Congress has failed to approve trade
agreements before, including the International Trade Organization
in 1950, the Organization for Trade Cooperation in 1956, and the

Antidumping Code in 1967.

Congress might go along with stronger rules, but only rules that others abide by. There is a widespread perception in Washington and in the U.S. public at large that other countries cheat. The playing field is not level. This accounts for the periodic attempts in Congress to rewrite U.S. unfair trade practices statutes. Every time they are rewritten, more practices are defined as unfair and further discretion is taken away from the President. He has no choice whether or not to impose countervailing duties. They are mandatory. A further tightening of the unfair trade statutes is likely to be part of the price paid for obtaining negotiating authority.

Trade legislation granting negotiating authority or implementing agreements is usually accompanied by other policy changes which Congress demands as its price for going along with the President's desire to negotiate. The passage of the Trade Expansion Act of 1962 came shortly after the Kennedy Administration had successfully negotiated the first textile agreements. In the 1962 Act Congress revised U.S. trade laws on the escape clause and passed the first trade adjustment assistance program for workers. Finally, because Congress felt that the State Department was giving too much weight to foreign policy considerations in its trade negotiations, it created a new office in the Executive Office of the President—the U.S. Special Trade Representative to serve as trade negotiator and as a broker between domestic interest groups and with Congress.

With the passage of the Trade Act of 1974 Congress went further in rewriting U.S. trade laws on unfair trade practices, lowering the threshold for injury on escape clauses, and substantially liberalizing adjustment assistance for workers. In the Trade Agreements Act of 1979 Congress went even further in removing Presidential discretion in the unfair trade statutes covering dumping and countervailing duties and in transferring the responsibility for enforcing the laws from Treasury to the Department of Commerce. Some attention will have to be paid to Congressional concerns in order to obtain the negotiating authority for the new round.

It would be easier to sell Congress on the need for new negotiations if Congress felt that progress could be made on issues with strong constituencies like agriculture, services or high technology. But getting these items on the agenda will not be easy. Progress will be harder.

Decisions on the domestic consensus will be constrained by the need to develop an international consensus. If it is to be a broad multilateral negotiation, key developing countries must be included. How can they be enticed to negotiate? They have shown little interest in services, trade-distorting investment practices, counterfeiting, intellectual property, and high technology. They seek greater market access in labor-intensive industries, textile liberalization, agriculture reforms, and stronger rules in some areas.

With these issues included, the development of a domestic consensus grows still harder. The political clout of the labor-intensive industries is substantial. Even the Reagan Administration, which fervently proclaims its support of free trade, has adopted more restrictive policies in textiles and steel. Greater market access will also raise adjustment problems in other labor-intensive industries.

As it now stands, Congress is unlikely to grant the President the continuing authority to negotiate unless services are on the agenda which, in turn, will require the United States to accept agenda items backed by other countries.[9] Key developing countries oppose negotiations on services in GATT but want their own issues put on the agenda. They may hold out for textiles and market access in other labor-intensive industries. The U.S. textile industry opposes new negotiations, preferring to focus its attention on renewing the Multifibre Agreement in 1986. If the politically sensitive industries, like textiles, are going to be on the table, passage of the next Trade Act will be extremely difficult and progress in negotiations even harder still.

Constraint: Adjustment Resistance

The steel and the textile/apparel industries provide, perhaps, the best examples of the political pressures to erect obstacles to adjustment.[10] Political pressure from both industries is intense. As a result, both industries drifted into regimes of managed trade. The lobbying clout of threatened U.S. industries could be a powerful constraint on the U.S. ability to compromise, once negotiations begin. Since they may have the power to block implementing legislation, their interests will have to be taken into account.

Textiles

Managed trade in textiles dates back to the early 1960s. Why has the textile and apparel industry been protected for so long? The number and geographic distribution of workers is one major reason. A majority of Congressional districts have some textile or apparel producers. Over 2.2 million workers in the United States (12 percent of the manufacturing labor force) are employed in textiles and apparel. Another major reason is that textile and apparel workers are, on average, disadvantaged in terms of their labor market experience. Furthermore, the industry is sometimes characterized as the "Third World in the United States" and as the domestic counterpart of U.S. immigration policy. English is not a prerequisite for a job.

The political clout of the industry is best indicated by the number of Congressional co-sponsors of the textile quota bill in 1985 which would roll back imports by 30 percent. Originally introduced to establish the industry's position prior to the renewal of the MFA in 1986, it attracted over 300 co-sponsors in the House and 60 in the Senate by September 1985. Evidence of textile industry influence also is reflected in the Reagan Administration's policies. As early as the 1980 campaign, the President promised Republican Senator Strom Thurmond of South Carolina that import growth would be related to growth in the domestic market. To follow through, in December 1983 the Administration promulgated a new administrative rule defining market disruption from uncontrolled sources. As a consequence, the number of "calls" alleging market disruption increased dramatically. In 1982, there were 39 calls; in 1983 there were 112, 52 of them in December; the pace continued with 110 calls in 1984 and 70 by July 1985.

In September 1984 the Administration again changed the administrative regulations for textiles, significantly tightening import quotas by country of origin. This move was aimed mainly at China, which the United States felt was transshipping products through intermediate countries. Retailers complained that the new regulation increased business uncertainty over the sources of supply. Agricultural interests, fearing Chinese retaliation might hit them, opposed the regulation but it went into effect.

Steel

Protection in the steel industry is also long standing. For security reasons, the United States needs a steel industry, but many U.S. plants are older and less efficient than those elsewhere, U.S. labor costs are higher, and for many years the industry ignored the implications of newer technologies on the industry. New plants could be built, but this would only increase unneeded world capacity. Europe is reorganizing its steel industry, cutting back and rationalizing its operations. Government intervention to achieve similar results are less practical in the United States. Consequently, for almost two decades, the United States has wrestled with how best to encourage adjustment and still protect the steel industry.

Trade restrictions on carbon steel began in 1969 with voluntary export restraints on steel imports from Europe and Japan. These restraints lasted in various forms until 1974. The trigger price mechanism based upon "fair value" and directed mainly at Japan was adopted in 1978. When imports from Europe continued to rise, a bilateral agreement restricting imports from the EC was concluded in 1982. In late 1984 bilateral agreements were extended to cover trade with Brazil, Mexico, South Korea, Argentina, and some smaller countries. It is not coincidental that bilateral steel accords are spreading. A similar phenomenon happened in textiles. When market conditions lessen an industry's competitiveness vis-à-vis the rest of the world, it is almost impossible to control imports from uncontrolled sources. In 1984 Ambassador Brock compared steel trade problems to a hydra's heads—as soon as you take care of one, another pops up.

In the fall of 1984 the political pressure pushing steel restrictions became apparent when 28 Senators and 222 Representatives co-sponsored bills introduced to restrict steel imports to 15 percent of the U.S. market. If this trend toward bilateral negotiations restricting trade in steel continues, an MFA (Multi Ferrous Arrangement) for steel could be on the horizon. Such regimes and the cartelization they engender are inimical to an open trading system. Once established, they are self-regulating and difficult to abolish.

When industries like steel and textiles are granted extended protection, it helps institutionalize protection in the executive branch. In effect, Congress delegates the authority both to negotiate and to regulate or manage trade in these industries; and when trade is managed, the nature of the government-business relationship changes. Today, in steel and textiles, trade is managed by a series of bilateral agreements between the United States and supplying countries which are negotiated by government civil servants whose careers may depend upon the outcome of negotiations. The Commerce, Labor and State Departments and the Office of the U.S. Trade Representative, all have appointed textile negotiators who generally share the same objectives.

Contributing further toward the restrictive bias, textile policy making is done outside of the normal mainstream of U.S. trade policy. Textile policy is not subject to automatic review by senior government officials from other agencies or sectors, like agriculture, which could be significantly affected by the result of those decisions. Nor do consumer groups, retailers or other interested groups have adequate opportunity for comment. The process is opaque; normal checks and balances are absent.

Constraint: The Reduction of Adjustment Assistance

As an alternative to protection and the major policy instrument to facilitate adjustment due to trade liberalization, the United States has relied since 1962 on a special adjustment assistance program for trade-displaced workers.[11] A proposal for a trade adjustment assistance (TAA) program was first brought into national prominence in 1954 by David McDonald, head of the steelworkers' union. As part of the package to ensure labor support for the Kennedy Round of multilateral trade negotiations, the Trade Expansion Act of 1962 established TAA for workers whose layoff could be attributed to a tariff reduction. The program provided compensation and adjustment services to trade-displaced workers. In 1974, TAA was liberalized to cover all cases where imports "contributed importantly" to worker displacement. This change helped to secure passage of the Trade Act of 1974 which gave the President authority to enter into the Tokyo Round negotiations.

In the early 1970s, free trade advocates, especially members of the business and academic communities, described TAA as "an integral part of U.S. trade policy." The big test of the program came in 1980 when the auto industry had over 250,000 layoffs and TAA outlays jumped to $1.7 billion from an annual average of $300 million earlier. The sharp increase in payments in 1980—81 focused public and policy-maker attention on the program and TAA came under intense criticism for being expensive, inefficient and inequitable. These criticisms provoked the Reagan Administration to make important legislative changes in the program during the budget reconciliation process in 1981.

Although program costs were expected to fall dramatically by 1982 as the auto industry, the major beneficiary, began to recover, the TAA program was restructured and several modifications were made in an attempt to reduce the program's inequities, inefficiencies and costs. Cumulatively, these changes lowered expenditures significantly while redressing some of the program's problems. The number of TAA recipients declined to 10 percent of the 1979—80 level. Critics argued that a commitment had been broken. Lane Kirkland, the head of the AFL-CIO, called the TAA cuts "... another broken promise to those who pay the price of trade liberalization."

With the increase in protectionist sentiment, there is renewed support for some form of trade adjustment assistance. Despite attempts to kill the program by the Reagan Administration, Congress has twice voted to extend it. The TAA program was due to expire at the end of September 1983, but on the last day of the month the program was extended for two more years without incorporating what had been learned about how the old program worked. Again, at the end of September 1985 when it was slated to be eliminated, Congress extended the program while debating whether to revitalize it. Even the Reagan Administration is considering revitalizing the program. For now, it remains a shell of its former self.

In an important sense, the reduction of trade adjustment assistance by the Reagan administration makes it more difficult for the United States to pursue free trade policies. In the past, displaced workers were compensated, which helped to mute the calls for protectionism. In its refusal to eliminate the program, Congress has demonstrated that TAA serves as a political alternative to import restrictions. TAA also provided the President with an intermediate option between import relief and no relief. Now that TAA is more limited and might be eliminated, it becomes politically more difficult to allow foreign importers, even if they are efficient and acting within the trading rules, to sell freely in the United States. At the same time, the threat used overseas by the Administration, that without new negotiations Congress will pass restrictive legislation, is more credible in the absence of the TAA support program.

Constraint: The Security Dimension

It may be true that "trade policy is foreign policy," but trade ministers win few debates with defense ministers.[12] The Reagan Administration entered office determined to strengthen America's military might and resist Soviet expansion and aggression. The Administration increased defense spending, to a remarkable extent, even if the budget deficit widened alarmingly in the process. However, the demands of a strong defense undermined the chances for a coherent trade policy and imposed significant constraints on U.S. trade negotiators seeking liberalization. The Japanese rightly ask, "how can you expect to be competitive, if you use your best minds on projects that are not allowed to reach the market place?" Three examples show how security policy constrains and distorts trade policy.

First, all Administrations are tempted to use trade as a stick to punish aggressors. It almost never works and usually irritates allies more than it chastises enemies. The Carter Administration embargoed grain shipments to the Soviet Union in the aftermath of the 1979 Afghanistan invasion. American farmers lost a large market. The Soviet Union, pausing not a moment, bought their grain from Argentina and other countries. When the Reagan Administration lifted the embargo, the Soviet Union returned to the U.S. market but also continued to buy elsewhere rather than depend on the United States as the sole supplier.[13] The lesson was not learned. After the Polish government broke the Solidarity movement, the Reagan Administration tried to stop the transfer to the Soviet Union of technology necessary to build a natural gas pipeline to Western Europe. Over nearly unanimous opposition from American business and European allies, the United States even forbade American companies from transferring technology to their foreign subsidiaries that might help the Soviet Union. It did not work. The Soviet Union developed the necessary technologies themselves—sooner than it would have otherwise. The Europeans, upset at the extraterritorial extension of U.S. law to subsidiaries of U.S. companies operating in their countries, redoubled their resolve not to depend just on the United States. They decided to develop key technologies themselves or bring in alternative suppliers from Japan. American business and American exports suffered.[14]

Second, even in "normal" times, the United States and other industrial countries try to limit the transfer of critical knowledge, technology and products to the Soviet Union. Export restraints are coordinated among NATO countries, but the United States is stricter and more bureaucratic than any other country in their enforcement. Some of the technology that is banned for export (e.g., until recently, IBM personal computers) is readily available from other sources. Moreover, export licenses are required not only for goods going to the Soviet Union and its allies, but also for goods being shipped to countries that might possibly re-export to U.S. enemies. And, even where export licenses are granted, numerous bureaucratic hurdles and delays often persuade buyers to shop elsewhere if the products are available. Although there are certainly good reasons for trying to limit the transfer of sensitive technologies to

America's adversaries, most businessmen find the present program ill-conceived and terribly managed. The net result may be to hurt legitimate U.S. exports much more than it hurts the Soviet Union and its allies.[15]

Third, the U.S. military spending on weapons and communications systems distorts even as it propels American innovation. Private contractors divert attention and resources to research with military applications instead of focusing on commercial problems. Even when this work leads to breakthroughs with commercial possibilities, the government often prevents it from being used in the marketplace for fear that it will end up in the Soviet Union. In other instances, American companies end up being very good at doing things that are not particularly useful. For example, it is rumored that U.S. firms are the best in the world at building vertical tunnels which might be useful for launching missiles after a first-strike nuclear attack. Unfortunately, Japanese and Italian firms are now superior to U.S. firms at building horizontal tunnels. As a result, foreign firms got the jobs of extending subway and sewer systems in New York and San Francisco. Some analysts fear that the Reagan Administration's Strategic Defense Initiative could further divert many of the best engineers and scientists away from commercially important projects. Europe, by participating in or emulating the American program, could lose ground in the technology race. Japan, which will continue to develop products for the marketplace, will thrive.

These security considerations have replaced the earlier concern which the United States had in the 1950s with the need to develop a strong, unified Europe as a counterweight to the Eastern bloc. At that time the United States was willing to sacrifice economic interests (e.g., in encouraging the formation of the EC) for security goals. Now the constraint is less direct but just as effective. U.S. commercial interests and objectives will clash with security and foreign policy objectives. Thus, trade policy continues to be a stepchild not only of domestic economic policies, but of foreign policy as well.

Outlook: Opportunity Seized or Lost?

Some countries want the goals and framework to be established before negotiations begin. This is a recipe for delay and failure. The discipline of negotiations is needed to force countries to tackle the complex problems of definition and measurement. The United

States is unlikely to articulate a trade strategy until forced by the start of negotiations. But some fundamental points can be listed now.

In the effort to establish a domestic consensus in the United States, there is a risk that the potential for progress may be exaggerated. Progress on agriculture, services and high technology will not come without major reciprocal concessions by the United States.

Agriculture is a perennial problem, but the budgetary consequences of huge support programs in Europe and the United States suggest that progress might be possible, if only to get credit for cutting expenditures. However, as the Administration was reminded in 1985 when it failed to pass its new farm bill, agriculture is highly political, so domestic progress will be glacial. For some time the major agriculture negotiations will be between Congress and the White House, not between the United States and its trading partners.

In services, high technology and trade-related investment issues, the United States is widely perceived by others to hold advantages. But service industries are heterogeneous and a conceptual framework for negotiations will be difficult to agree upon.[16] The definition, issues and goals for high technology are even less well understood. Progress will be slow.

Although liberalization and greater discipline in services and high technology could contribute to higher world-wide economic growth in the future, the obstacles to progress are formidable. Telecommunications in most countries is provided by self-regulating, government-owned or controlled monopolies. And the developing countries are reticent because they see these sectors as the "commanding heights" of their economies. If services are the leading edge of future growth and the source of most new employment, industrial and developing countries alike want to retain control of these sectors.

All nations want growth. If the aim of the new round is to maximize future economic growth, all nations will have to put the difficult issues—the sacred cows—on the table for negotiation. (Whether concessions can be won is another issue.) If the Reagan Administration is serious about strengthening the trading system and extending its discipline to new issues, domestic labor-adjustment problems caused by trade liberalization in labor-intensive industries will have to be addressed.

The Administration maintains that it is better to hold multilateral talks than to risk Congress taking unilateral actions. To protect against unrealistic expectations and to minimize domestic opposition from import-sensitive industries, the Administration has lowered its sights and is claiming that the next round will not be a major liberalizing effort. Rather than talking about the benefits which are derived from trade liberalization, it is talking only about stronger rules and discipline. But the negotiation of better rules is not necessarily neutral. If the United States could not get its way when it was the dominant hegemonic power, what can it expect to get today? To get the rules it wants, the United States will have to accept some things that other countries want.

If new rules are the only harvest, these new negotiations could become the ultimate test of the bicycle theory. In simple terms, a rule-making round is not sexy enough to hold the interest of industry and the attention of high-level political leaders for what could be a decade of negotiations. Furthermore, Congress is frustrated. Unless sufficient progress is achieved, Congress might fail to ratify the final agreement and the dissolution of the multilateral system could follow. Or if Congress does go along with new rules, it is likely to attach a few conditions of its own to the implementing legislation. Reciprocity in the narrow sense of tit-for-tat on a bilateral basis is gaining currency in Congress. Congress might mandate that the President take aggressive reciprocal action if others do not follow the rules.

The successful completion of the negotiations will hinge upon strong, effective U.S. leadership at the highest levels. That leadership will be needed at home, in dealing with Congress, and overseas, with other heads of state. Overseas, there is considerable doubt about the U.S. commitment to trade liberalization and stronger international discipline. The transfer of William Brock from U.S. Trade Representative to Secretary of Labor in March 1985 raises doubts about the depth of President Reagan's commitment to trade negotiations. Highly respected at home and abroad, Brock was the most senior trade minister in the world and the point man in the Administration's effort to launch new trade negotiations. His successor, Clayton Yeutter, is well respected overseas as a former deputy trade representative, but his ability to build the domestic consensus and to work with Congress is unknown.

The U.S. trade embargo of Nicaragua and rejection of the competence of the World Court of Justice in a complaint brought by Nicaragua raise questions about the U.S. willingness to abide by stronger international disciplines. To paraphrase a comment by one high-level European trade official to one of the authors, "The U.S. is always holier-than-thou about strengthening international discipline until they have to do something that they find politically unacceptable. Then the U.S. ignores its responsibilities. Why should anybody believe the U.S. will act any differently in the future?"

The Tokyo Round of negotiations was floundering in 1977 until Robert Strauss, with the strong backing of Jimmy Carter and with his extensive political connections as former head of the Democratic National Committee, entered the arena. Overseas, Strauss was perceived as a strong negotiator with a mandate from the President to complete the negotiations. At home, Strauss negotiated with interest groups and built a domestic consensus which lost only four votes in the Senate and seven votes in the House in 1979 when the agreement was approved. Two years earlier, the legislation had not been given much chance to pass at all. What remains to be seen is whether the Reagan Administration and its successors will have the commitment and the resolve to pull off a successful negotiation in both the domestic and international arenas.

Notes

1. Kevin Phillips, "The Politics of Protectionism," *Public Opinion* (April/May 1985), pp. 41—46.

2. Reports to this effect began to appear in 1980. See *President's Report on U.S. Competitiveness*, Office of Foreign Economic Research, U.S. Department of Labor (Washington, D.C.: GPO, 1980). The recently completed President's Commission on Industrial Competitiveness *Global Competition: The New Reality* (Washington, D.C.: GPO, 1985) came to a similar conclusion. These reports also address the myriad other factors held to be responsible for the deterioration of the U.S. competitive position including poor management, poor quality, expensive labor, etc.

3. Importers and exporters believe they understand their interests as they relate to trade policy. Only a few business leaders worried about or understood international monetary policy until recently; see E.E. Schattschneider, *Politics, Pressure and the Tariff* (New York: Prentice Hall, Inc., 1935) and Raymond Bauer, Ithiel Pool and Louis Dexter, *American Business and Public Policy: The Politics of Foreign Trade* (New York: Atherton Press, 1967). I.M. Destler, *System Under Stress* (Washington, D.C.: Institute for International Economics, forthcoming 1985) provides an up-to-date analysis of the trade-policy process.

4. See "The Chairmen's Report on A New Round of Multilateral Trade Negotiations," submitted to the U.S. Trade Representative, May 15, 1985. In the words of the report, "there is a strong correlation between the level of commitment to bringing new areas under the GATT and the strength of support for a new MTN."

5. Ibid.

6. After the problems involved in getting the Kennedy Round negotiations ratified, Congress included fast-track procedures in the Trade Act of 1974, which require Congressional consideration within 60 days of submission. During that period, Congress can only vote the measure up or down, no amendments are in order. See Robert Pastor, *Congress and the Politics of U.S. Foreign Economic Policy* (Berkeley: University of California Press, 1980).

7. Speech before the National Press Club, April 25, 1985.

8. "The New Global Economy: First Steps in a United States Trade Strategy," Preliminary Report of the Senate Democratic Working Group on Trade Policy, April 1985.

9. This was underscored in the Trade And Tariff Act of 1984 which authorizes the President to give high priority to the negotiation of agreements covering trade in services.

10. For an analysis of adjustment in textiles and steel, see C. Michael Aho, "U.S. Labor Market Adjustment and Import Restrictions," in Ernest Preeg, ed., *Hard Bargaining Ahead: U.S. Trade Policy and the Developing Countries* (New Brunswick, NJ: Transaction Books, for Overseas Development Council, 1985), pp. 87—111.

11. For an extended discussion of the rationales for and an evaluation of the U.S. Trade Adjustment Assistance Program, see C. Michael Aho and Thomas O. Bayard, "The Costs and Benefits of Trade Adjustment Assistance" in Robert Baldwin and Anne O. Krueger, eds., *The Structure and Evolution of Recent U.S. Trade Policy* (Chicago: National Bureau of Economic Research and University of Chicago Press, 1984), pp. 153—91.

12. Richard Cooper, "Trade Policy is Foreign Policy," *Foreign Policy*, no. 9 (Winter 1972—73), pp. 18—36.

13. See I.M. Destler, *Making Foreign Economic Policy* (Washington: Brookings Institution, 1980) and Gary Clyde Hufbauer and Jeffrey Schott, *Economic Sanctions Reconsidered: History and Current Policy* (Washington: Institute for International Economics, 1985).

14. This is not a new issue. Irritation over United States extraterritorial extension of its laws and control over U.S. business has rankled Europe and Canada for decades. Thane Gustafson, "The Soviet Gas Campaign: Politics and Policy in Soviet Decisionmaking" (Santa Monica, CA: Rand Corporation, 1983).

15. Stories abound of instances where U.S. firms got technology they needed from Soviet sources which had obtained them in the United States. More generally, there is the problem of America's tendency to shoot itself in the foot. For example, the Foreign Corrupt Practices Act, however good its intentions, often has the effect of preventing U.S. firms from getting foreign business that they could have won by following accepted behavior in other countries. Or, despite all the commotion over the U.S. trade deficit with Japan, American law prevents the sale of Alaskan oil to Japan.

16. An early effort to set out such a conceptual framework by the U.S. is William Brock, "A Simple Plan for Negotiating Trade in Services," *The World Economy*, vol. 5, no. 3 (November 1982), pp. 229—40. Fleshing out this plan will pose an immense challenge to negotiators.

Five

Other Industrial Countries

The European Community, Japan and the United States are the three pillars of the trading system. No multilateral trade agreement is possible without them. With Canada, they compose the Quadrilateral which has met periodically since 1983 to discuss trade issues. Australia, Sweden and other industrial country members of the 24-nation OECD sometimes propose compromises and move issues forward as well. What follows is a breakdown of the domestic constraints and trade priorities of the leading countries. We include Canada because of its Quadrilateral status, but omit middle-level powers even though these may help fashion bargains later.

European Community

High unemployment rates and a stagnant economic outlook plague the Community. Since it is easier politically to blame these failings on scapegoats beyond one's borders than to change deeply embedded social policies, the Community could become the most significant obstacle to maintaining open markets and further liberalizing trade.

Although Europe has suffered through a prolonged recession since 1981, its employment problems are structural, not cyclical. Between 1973 and 1985 no new net jobs were created in the Community and unemployment rates have increased monotonically.[1] In the best growth years of the 1960s and 1970s, West European employment only expanded by 300,000. Most Europeans believe the prospects for future employment are bleak because the pace of structural change is accelerating just when Europe's "baby boom" generation is adding up to one million new workers to the labor force annually.[2]

Furthermore, European unemployment rates are likely to stay high because of labor market inflexibility. Strict job protection laws and generous unemployment insurance benefits discourage new hiring and help make unemployment rates among new entrants to

77

the labor force more than double the overall unemployment rate in most European countries. Worse still, medium-term forecasts predict growth rates insufficient to absorb enough people into the work force to reduce unemployment in the Community. (The OECD forecasts European unemployment above 11 percent through 1986.)

Another factor which will increase the probability of international conflict is the discrepancy in adjustment capabilities among the major industrial countries. The convergence of their industrial structures, growing competition in many sectors from the developing countries, and continued rapid technological change all heighten the need for flexible and efficient adjustment. Even prior to the onset of the world-wide recession in 1981 Europe was not performing as well as Japan or the United States. Between 1970 and 1980 both the United States and Japan generated nine jobs for every ten entrants into the labor force while the Western European economies created only about four new jobs for each ten new entrants. Slow adjustment to change increases the pressure on governments to intervene to protect workers, thus making international trade and trade policy conflicts more probable.

Several factors explain Europe's difficulty in adjusting: First, Europe does not have a unified common market. Labor mobility is limited for cultural and national reasons; language barriers inhibit many pan-European ventures. National markets are segmented and in critical areas, like telecommunications, they are highly regulated at the national level.[3] Industrial restructuring in basic industries is hampered by the need to get the unanimous agreement of the EC member-states. This ensures that restructuring in the Community moves at the pace of the slowest. And, with the admission of Spain and Portugal, the Community is going to become even more heterogeneous and less integrated. Obtaining internal agreement on trade negotiating positions and on the pace of industrial restructuring will get harder.[4]

Second, in most European countries the government plays a large, pervasive role in the economy. There is a high degree of regulation at the national level. Government as a share of GNP is higher in all the major European countries than in either Japan or the United States. The attitude of government toward entrepreneurial ventures is also less conducive to the generation of new businesses. Bankruptcy statutes are punitive. By contrast, bankruptcy is treated less harshly in the United States and Japan, with Japan leading the United States in the annual number of bankruptcies. European capital markets do not provide venture capital in the same volume as capital markets do in the United States. This makes it more difficult for entrepreneurs in the emerging high-technology industries to obtain sufficient funding to launch new businesses.

Third, wage and labor market flexibility are more limited in Europe. Collective bargaining is largely done at the national level by the "social partners," in contrast with the decentralized industry and craft bargaining in the United States or the enterprise bargaining in Japan. Job protection statutes are so stringent that they require up to two years severance pay for firms laying off workers. This discourages the hiring of additional employees and the formation of new enterprises. Employment growth is already inhibited by the high non-wage labor costs used to fund social programs and the generous cost-of-living escalators for labor. From 1973 to 1983, real labor costs per employee grew by 2.1 percent per annum in the Community as compared with only 0.5 percent in the United States.

Fourth, slower overall growth in the Community means that new displacements or new entrants are not absorbed into the employment ranks. This heightens the political importance of labor issues and increases the probability that additional government measures will be taken to ameliorate the problem. The proliferation of political parties in many countries and the fragility of the ruling coalitions means that government leaders must tread carefully on initiatives such as trade liberalization, which might add to labor adjustment problems.

Fifth is agriculture. The support program for the agricultural sector, the Common Agriculture Policy (CAP), is one of the major political deals underlying the European Community—the glue holding together the EC. Furthermore, continued support programs are critical for several ruling coalition governments within the EC. Responding to the high support prices that they have been able to obtain, politically powerful European farmers produce enormous surpluses of food. These surpluses are being generated, at an enormous cost to the EC budget, behind variable import levies, and then are often dumped on world markets. But even though the CAP may cost billions of dollars a year, lead to distortions in world agriculture markets, and provoke continual disputes with the United States, the EC believes that it must hold fast in support of the CAP.

Apart from these adjustment difficulties, which will burden the Community as it prepares for and participates in the new round, the EC will also be hampered by its cumbersome administrative processes for reaching decisions. The EC has had to develop an elaborate system for reaching positions, taking decisions, and conducting negotiations. The European Commission, not the individual states, represents the EC in negotiations. The Commission is the internal executive committee of the EC, but it must have approval from the Council of Ministers, which is the organ which exercises sovereign control by the member states. The Council of Ministers draws up a mandate for the Commission, which does the actual negotiations. A separate committee made up of representatives from capitals oversees the Commission's negotiations in each functional area.

Interest groups have input at both the national and Community level, but they are less influential than in the United States. They are less influential at the national level because the member states have a broader agenda of issues that they must balance among each other and often cannot accede to national interest group demands. At the Community level, the interest groups are dealing with the bureaucracy, not directly with elected officials who are more likely to side with particular interests. Still, when one government is firmly committed to a position, it can have a disproportionate effect upon the final outcome.

Just like other Community decisions, trade negotiating positions are arrived at by consensus. Since unanimity is required, decisions are usually reached with difficulty, rendering the Community's position inflexible and, often on the basis of the lowest common denominator. Gardner Patterson, a former Deputy Director-General of GATT, states that "the Community's behavior creates serious problems and threatens [the] international trading system. . . It can be traced to the structure of the EC decision-making process, which is slow, hard to predict and has a protectionist bias."[5]

Reaching negotiating positions is further complicated by the increasing use of nontariff barriers by many EC countries. Many of these barriers arose out of individual national attempts to cope with slow growth and rising unemployment. The barriers are not handled on a Community basis, but negotiations restricting certain practices will require a Community position during the negotiations.

Under these circumstances, it is easy to see the Community's reluctance to move forward with new trade negotiations. And it also explains why "European rigidities" have become an issue of concern outside Europe.[6]

In summary, Europe has two problems which lead to a

dilemma. Problem number one is jobs or, more accurately, the lack of them. Unemployment, underemployment and problems of adjustment afflict the Continent. Any trade concessions that cost Europe jobs without an immediate promise of creating more jobs will run into a stone wall of opposition from the start.

Problem number two is agriculture, which is viewed as the constitutional bedrock on which the Community stands and is therefore untouchable (although the admission of Spain and Portugal will be certain to strain the financial resources and creativity of the Community to devise stop-gap measures to maintain unanimity on the CAP.)

The dilemma involves liberalization. Bureaucrats in Brussels, business, and political leaders throughout Europe recognize that no single European country has a market large enough to provide economies of scale for large European companies. Without an integrated European market, European companies are probably doomed to be less efficient and competitive than their U.S. or Japanese counterparts. This is particularly true in high-technology areas. IBM and Citibank, for example, are already more European in structure and planning than any European high-technology firm or bank. Few European firms can compete effectively with them across the board.[7] The dilemma is: can Europe liberalize and eventually eliminate barriers among its states while simultaneously liberalizing access to Europe for non-European firms? Or, must it protect against foreign interests as it liberalizes internally?

In short, Euro-pessimism is fashionable and has considerable justification. And now there is renewed talk of a technological gap not only between the United States and Europe, but between Europe and Japan. This has spurred attempts by the Community to enhance competitiveness in high-technology sectors by establishing technology consortia. French President Mitterand's push for a European R&D effort (EUREKA) in response to the U.S. Strategic Defense Initiative is but one example.

Given the internal economic problems of record unemployment, burgeoning farm subsidies and lagging competitiveness in technically sophisticated industries, the Community will have an extremely difficult time reaching consensus on the mandate for and conduct of a new round. Such internal discord in the Community delayed progress in the Kennedy Round and it is likely to happen again.[8]

To complicate matters further, it is hard to find areas in which the Community is eager to change much. It could gain in some of the services sectors and on counterfeiting and intellectual property. Greater market access to Japan and the LDCs would also be a benefit. And, to the extent that extending and strengthening the GATT system assured its continued functioning, the EC would benefit along with all other countries.

But on agriculture, safeguards, institutional reform, and market access, the Community has been virtually isolated in past international negotiations. Agriculture already has been cited. On safeguards, the Community adamantly insisted on selectivity during the Tokyo Round until the negotiations finally broke down. Although other countries came close to agreeing to a watered-down form of "consensual" selectivity, it came too late to get a change in instructions from Brussels. On institutional reform, the Community has always favored ad hoc political deals instead of the United States' preference for establishing and strengthening rules, dispute-settlement mechanisms, and surveillance procedures. Finally, the Community, like the United States and Japan, will be pressed by domestic producers in textiles and in other industries that sustain high barriers to trade not to liberalize.

Unless there is a change either in the economic outlook or in the domestic politics of trade within the Community, developing an acceptable package will be difficult. Minimizing damage will not be sufficient. Positive gains are essential.

Still, not everyone is a Euro-pessimist, and many in Europe see trade talks as a way to bring external pressure to bear on the Community and the individual member states to liberalize and to reform some of the practices that are retarding its economic performance. The challenge, as in other countries, will be to mobilize sufficient support in the private sector from those interests that would gain from trade liberalization.

Japan

"Bashing" Japan has become a popular world-wide sport. The major constraint on Japan is that it has done too well, not too poorly under the current trading system. Japan never seems to buy significant amounts of manufactured goods from abroad even as its manufactured exports of everything from automobiles to semiconductors seem to increase every year. As a result, Japan has three choices. First, it can persuade the rest of the world that it is playing by the rules (which is an incentive for Japan to support strengthening the rules). Second, it can import more manufactured goods from the rest of the world. Third, it can limit its own exports or have them limited by others.

One explanation of Japan's success is that Japanese workers and society are harder working and better organized than anybody else—that they build better mousetraps at cheaper prices. Nobody outside Japan wants to believe this explanation. Other factors that might account for Japan's recent trading success are reviewed below.

First, there is the traditional trade theory explanation: Japan had to export in order to import the raw materials it lacked.[9] Japan lacks natural resources and necessarily runs a significant deficit on its trade in resources. Japanese and many American analysts contend that even if Japan did everything that the United States, Europe and the developing countries demanded, it would still run large trade surpluses in manufactured products with the rest of the world.[10]

Second, Japanese citizens have a high propensity to save. This means that there is a low absorptive capacity in the Japanese market. The small size of most Japanese homes and traditional Japanese preferences for uncluttered living may also contribute to the low Japanese demand for foreign goods. Because of its high savings rate, Japan does not absorb all that it produces; the remainder is available for export, and the excess savings (over investment) is available for foreign lending.[11]

Third, the Japanese consumers are suspicious of new producers, particularly foreign ones. The "old-boy" network is so well established in Japan that it is difficult for newcomers, even new Japanese firms, to break into existing markets.[12] Foreign firms can sell in Japan, as is shown by the success of firms like IBM and Coca Cola.[13] But, patience over a number of years and a willingness to adapt products to suit Japanese tastes are usually required. Even a direct plea to buy foreign products from Prime Minister Nakasone in early 1985 had little apparent persuasive appeal to his constituents. Furthermore, Japanese consumers tend to be extremely loyal, making it hard for foreign firms to take business away from established domestic companies. As a result, even if foreign firms are allowed to enter the Japanese market only after domestic firms establish themselves, gaining a large share of the Japanese market becomes harder. This allows Japanese firms to take a longer-term view of their business and not to worry so much about the short term.

Fourth, Japan's economy is organized differently from those of its major trading partners. GATT was not structured with Japan in mind but on the basis of Anglo-American assumptions about the desirability of limited government intervention and unfettered competition. Japan's elaborate bureaucratic process, staffed by a first-rate civil service, the structure of corporate relationships, and the nature of interaction between government and business suggest to outside observers a pervasive effect upon the economy and trade flows. That the structure of corporate-government relationships could significantly affect a country's propensity to export and import was not seriously considered by GATT's founders, and GATT deals with it only tangentially today.[14]

Fifth, as everywhere else, Japanese politics constrains the ability of the government to increase imports. The conservative Liberal Democratic Party (LDP) has ruled Japan since the war. Rural based, its majority in the Diet has shrunk in recent elections. The LDP has generally resisted efforts to increase urban representation, and to reinforce the loyalty of its local leaders, the LDP has recently decentralized its nominating and selection processes. At present, the factions within the LDP (notably those associated with Tanaka and Fukuda) are positioning themselves to push their candidates to succeed Nakasone as Prime Minister in 1986.

The complexities of internal LDP politics work against liberalization of entry into Japan. Prime Minister Nakasone, despite great personal popularity in Japan, represents a small faction of the LDP and does not have tremendous power within the party. Despite his promises to open up the Japanese market, his ability to deliver is hampered by his weak standing. Diet members are more sensitive to their constituents involved with citrus, beef, tobacco products and wood products than with would-be importers. They are much more concerned that local telephone calls remain at 10 yen (about 5¢, or about one-third of what it costs NTT to provide the service) than with the wishes of foreign data-processing services and telephone-equipment providers. So long as those who vote for them do not want to buy foreign goods and services, most LDP members will resist forcing imports on them. (A 1985 Japanese poll of consumers found that 53 percent had purchased foreign goods in the past few years, but only 23 percent said they would cooperate with the government's call for increased use of imports.)

In one important respect decision-making in Japan is more efficient than in the United States or the EC. As a parliamentary system, Japan does not suffer from struggles between different branches of government. The struggles occur primarily within the bureaucracy.

Sixth, bureaucratic turf battles in the Japanese government are particularly fierce. The Foreign Affairs Ministry, Finance, Agriculture, the Ministry of International Trade and Industry (MITI), and the Ministry of Post and Telecommunications (MPT) all work for their particular constituencies. The government bureaucracy in Japan is staffed by the crème de la crème of Japanese university graduates, who are accorded much more respect and given much more responsibility than their counterparts in the United States or at the European Commission. Foreign economic policy is much more a matter of bureaucratic governance in Japan. Recent fights between MITI and MPT over telecommunications standards and rules are indicative of the tensions which exist on policy in technically advanced sectors. Even though Japan's parliamentary style is more efficient in its foreign economic negotiations than is either the United States or Europe, Japan found it necessary to establish a special section in the Prime Minister's office during the Tokyo Round to coordinate policy and handle domestic problems arising from the negotiations. Bureaucratic infighting could hamper Japanese negotiating flexibility in the coming round because the internal and external pressures on Japan will be greater. The Japanese may have more trouble holding their domestic consensus together because the rest of the world will not be as polite to Japan as in the past.

Seventh, and the most important to foreign critics, the Japanese government clearly devises rules that inhibit imports and promote exports. At the GATT Ministerial Meeting in November 1982, the then Japanese trade minister forthrightly claimed that Japan was the most open market in the world. He pointed out that tariffs on products entering Japan were on average lower than those in the United States or Europe. Still, Japanese procedures and standards are often designed to exhaust all but the largest and most determined foreign firms wishing to sell in Japan. Today, on a percentage basis, Japan imports fewer manufactured products from industrial and developing countries than it did ten or twenty years ago. Since 1970, Japanese imports of manufactured products from developing countries as a percentage of total industrial-country imports of LDC manufactured goods have declined significantly. In 1984, Japan bought only 8 percent of total OECD imports of LDC manufactured products, compared with 28 percent for the EC and 58 percent for the United States.

Many foreign firms and governments believe that whatever the appearance of procedural liberalization, they will somehow be prevented from competing fairly to sell their goods and services in Japan. This attitude is evident in the U.S. Congress today. When after years of frustration on citrus, beef, tobacco and wood products a new set of problems surrounding telecommunications equipment and value-added networks arose, Congress expressed its exasperation by unilaterally defining what is unfair—Japan is unfair![15] Similarly, the EC had in 1983 filed a GATT case which claimed that Japan had "nullified and impaired" its benefits under GATT. Japan often counters these attacks by pointing out that it is sending its export earnings back to its trading partners in the form of massive outward investment. If the overall flow of funds and not just the balance of trade is considered, Japan's contribution to world economic growth and stability is quite different.

On the export side, Japan (and MITI) are variously praised or condemned for their successful targeting of foreign markets in specific sectors. The Japanese argue that they provide products of excellent quality at competitive prices and that their servicing and attention to detail are superior. Japan's competitors admit that the products are usually well made and adapted to specific markets, but they charge that Japanese business and government collude unfairly. Even though Japanese firms compete actively with one another for business, producers who must compete with Japanese exports complain that the Japanese government gives their exporters more help and direction than is fair. Complaints run the gamut from dumping, to unfair subsidization, to overly favorable financing, to planned targeting in the absence of antitrust enforcement. They contend that Japanese firms build up huge economies of scale in their closed home market which helps them sell overseas. By the time foreign firms finally crack the Japanese market, Japanese firms have won the struggle in Japan and elsewhere. In short, it does not help foreign firms much if Japan removes barriers to entry after Japanese firms are solidly established in a given sector.[16]

Eighth, Japan spends very little on its own defense. The Japanese government focuses its research-and-development efforts on technologies that have direct commercial applications. Their success record is not perfect, but it is not surprising that the Japanese government is more efficient at helping produce products for the market place than other industrial-country governments are. Government funding goes further when it is used to develop products for the marketplace. Japanese companies, unlike their competitors, do not have to depend on spillovers from classified military work to fuel much of their commercial product development.

What can Japan be expected to do to deflect criticism from its manufactured goods trade surplus? Japan's order of preference would appear to be: (1) work to strengthen international trade rules under the GATT and demonstrate a commitment to abide by these rules; at the same time, continue to institute incremental liberalization of rules and procedures that hamper foreign exports to Japan; (2) where resistance to Japanese exports is high, agree to limit exports voluntarily; (3) set and meet targets of imports into Japan by sectors.

Although Japan is the continuous object of complaints from its trading partners in bilateral consultations, other industrial countries have not ganged up on Japan in multilateral fora. Wherever possible, the Japanese strategy in multilateral gatherings has been to stay at the sidelines while others argued among themselves. Thus, at the Bonn Summit of heads of state in early May 1985, Japan escaped the limelight. Prime Minister Nakasone was constructive and engaging while at the same time steering conversation away from Japanese trade and monetary policy issues. Similarly, at the GATT Ministerial Meeting in November 1982, the Japanese escaped unscathed when negotiations took a triangular structure among the United States, Europe and the LDCs. It is not surprising, therefore, that Japan is a strong supporter of new trade talks.

Japan usually supports efforts to improve and strengthen the system so long as they do not require substantial Japanese concessions or costs. On the subject of multilateral negotiations, including the extension of the GATT to new areas such as services, the Japanese were early and consistent supporters of U.S. efforts. Indeed, Prime Minister Nakasone was the first head of state publicly to call for a new round of trade talks. This deflected criticism, made them appear as cooperative actors in the trading system, and cost them practically nothing.

Japan realizes that efforts to keep the trading system reasonably open help it maintain access to its important export markets. Japanese leaders seem to believe they can continue to open their markets procedurally without substantial worry that they will be flooded by foreign imports. Cultural or linguistic and other invisible barriers to imports into Japan will persist even as Japan dismantles explicit barriers. Moreover, once negotiations begin, they are likely to last a long time.

The Japanese, more than other nations, understand that they will have as much opportunity as they need to shape the direction and scope of negotiations and therefore are unlikely to be hurt by them. Multilateral negotiations could in fact delay the necessity of making significant concessions in bilateral negotiations. Moreover, Japan shows signs of becoming a major service exporter. In 1984, for the first time, it showed a surplus in trade in services with the United States.[17] A system of rules and procedures for services, however general, could help foster Japan's expanding service export industry. Therefore, Japan is eager to support efforts to launch the new trade round and will play a significant role in its preparation and conduct.

The Japanese, as the second largest trading nation in the world and the one with the largest overall trade surplus, have an incentive to make certain that the system remains open, flexible, and strong. On some issues, Japan may even decide to take the lead independently during new negotiations. Japan will not replace the United States as the dominant trading power, but like the United States it has an incentive to take a longer-term view of the benefits of an open trading system. When specific concessions are sought, Japan will plead difficult domestic political realities along with everybody else.

This time, however, Japan will probably not get off so easily. The rest of the world is growing impatient. Fair or not, Japan is under growing pressure to change its ways and reduce its trade surplus. Frustrated competitors around the world are asking their own governments to provide equivalent support (as Korea is already doing) or that the Japanese government be persuaded to cut back its support and curb its companies. In addition, European countries have severely limited access to their markets for many Japanese products. For example, Italy virtually bars the importation of Japanese cars; and France, for a time, forced all Japanese video recorders to enter through the inland port of Poitiers and mandated that each one should be individually inspected. On the other side, many European firms have abandoned serious efforts to export to Japan. They believe that whatever the product, price, and quality, the Japanese will find ways to prevent them from successfully selling very much in Japan. The Americans have negotiated a series of voluntary export restraint (VER) agreements with the Japanese. Yet when the agreement on automobiles was lifted in March 1985, Japanese exports increased dramatically and American officials fumed.

On market access, Japan is in a better position to liberalize than any of the other major countries because its growth rate is higher and its unemployment rate is lower. This suggests that Japan has less to fear from trade liberalization than the United States or Europe. Labor adjustment problems are not as significant in Japan. Multilateral pressure could be brought to bear on Japan to do more to liberalize. But the other countries should not forget that liberalization benefits most those that practice it. Japan's efforts to liberalize should be emulated.

In the absence of significantly higher Japanese imports, Japan will either have to further curb its exports or it will be done for them. (Not surprisingly, the Japanese resent and fear such threats.) For some time now, U.S. officials have repeatedly pressured Japan to buy more U.S. products and services. Japanese officials have retreated step-by-step by making procedural concessions. But, in the U.S. and European views, nothing much has really changed—Japan's manufactured good surplus continues to rise.

Unless and until things do start to change in real terms, pressure on Japan, in bilateral and multilateral fora, will increase.

Canada

Canada's dilemma is clear. It is one side of the largest bilateral trade relationship in the world, totaling almost $120 billion annually. In 1984, Canada's exports to the United States topped $65 billion. The United States was the market for 73 percent of all Canadian exports, accounting for over 20 percent of Canada's GNP. Canada walks a tightrope. It wants and needs to increase trade with the United States and almost inevitably concurs with the United States on the desirability of a new trade round. At the same time, Canadians take great pains to remind the United States that they are a sovereign nation and not simply a northern extension of U.S. territory and policies.

Although Canada's economic performance over the past several years has been poor, compared to the United States, Canada's trade surplus with the United States has grown and, on a per capita basis, is now significantly larger than Japan's. Both the government in Ottawa and provincial governments want to maintain and, if possible, expand their access to the U.S. market. Large Canadian firms are willing to compete head on with American firms in Canada so long as they are guaranteed continued access to the much larger

American market.

Periodically, proposals surface for special bilateral trade arrangements. The Canadian-American Auto Pact of 1965 is one example. In 1982—83, the Trudeau government proposed discussion of a free trade area in several industries, and bilateral discussions began but quickly bogged down. The private sector has even gotten involved. In 1983, the Royal Bank of Canada took the initiative of proposing free trade in computer services between Canada and the United States.[18] Both governments expressed sincere interest but have chosen thus far to look at an even broader approach.

At their summit meeting in March 1985, President Reagan and Prime Minister Mulroney agreed to explore the possibility of a comprehensive bilateral free trade arrangement. The initiative was given further impetus by the release of a Canadian Royal Commission report in September 1985 which called for a comprehensive free trade arrangement between the two countries. The Commission argued that Canada would "benefit substantially from bilateral free trade with the United States, particularly from access to the expanded unrestricted market and from economies of scale."[19] Although the Commission was set up under the liberal Trudeau government, the ruling conservatives have also embraced the idea.

In late September 1985, Prime Minister Mulroney indicated his government's interest in pursuing a special bilateral trading arrangement with the United States. He argued, "Economics, geography, common sense and the national interest dictate that we try to secure and expand our trade with our closest and largest partner...We seek to negotiate the broadest possible package of mutually beneficial reductions in tariff and nontariff barriers between the two countries." Consciously avoiding the phrase "free trade" he went on to say "We need a better, a fairer and a more predictable trade relationship with the United States. At stake are more than two million jobs which depend on Canadian access to the U.S. market." The Reagan Administration reacted positively but did not immediately begin the formal discussion with Congress and the private sector which is required under U.S. law.[20]

Canada has historically been reluctant to forge stronger links with the United States for internal political reasons, not the least of which is that Canada is one-tenth as large.[21] But the increasing protectionist mood in the U.S. Congress worries Canadians that U.S. trade policy actions will turn against the entire world, including Canada. A bilateral pact could give Canada greater and more secure access to the U.S. market. For its part, the United States believes that stronger bilateral agreements with Canada would demonstrate to others the benefits and desirability of new agreements and, it is hoped, encourage others to join in on a multilateral basis. Over 75 percent of the trade between the two countries enters duty free, so that the substantive work will be on NTBs and new areas like services, investment, and intellectual property. A bilateral pact covering these issues could pioneer similar agreements in a broader, multilateral context. We say more about a possible U.S.-Canadian bilateral deal in Chapter 7.

Canada has been a strong supporter of GATT since its inception. In the new round, Canada, like the United States, wants progress on agriculture, safeguards, subsidies, services, and nontariff barriers. In addition, Canada has a specific interest in promoting freer trade in raw and semiprocessed products. In return, Canada is willing to live with the discipline and constraints that these new, stronger agreements would force on its industries.

In essence, Canada's position on the desirability of a new round is almost as strong as the United States'. Canada is far more enthusiastic about the need for negotiations to begin now than the Europeans are. At the same time, Canada has made it clear that on specific issues it will inevitably disagree with the United States. (One area of past disagreement was foreign investment policy.) The differences, however, are almost entirely about the details of substance and emphasis and not about the need to move the process along or about the overall agenda that needs to be addressed.

Canada, like Japan, also has a parliamentary system which increases its efficiency in international trade negotiations, although it is constrained somewhat by its federal form of government that gives the provinces important powers. Canada provides an interesting comparison with the other three major actors' internal decision-making procedures. Multilateral trade negotiations require changes in the institutional framework in which domestic decisions are reached, and they expose those groups which are most necessary to bring along during negotiations.[22] In the United States, the major constituents are business and labor, acting through Congress and the sectoral advisory committees. In the European Community, the member governments are the major constituents and, behind them, the private sector. In Japan, it is the bureaucracy. In Canada, the provinces are the major constituent parts.

During the Tokyo Round, Canada established a Canadian Coordinator for Trade Negotiations not only to improve the communication between the government and its negotiating team in Geneva and coordination within the federal bureaucracy, but, most important, to improve coordination between the federal bureaucracy and the provincial bureaucracies. Such an arrangement will no doubt be used again. To the extent that issues have large regional impacts, say, on raw materials or lumber, Canada's flexibility will be reduced. The need to gain assent will also diminish the Canadian government's flexibility in its bilateral negotiations with the United States.

***

Each of the Quadrilateral partners is saddled with serious domestic constraints on flexibility in the coming negotiations. In the United States, business and Congressional consensus are absent. Adjustment is causing severe strains, and the Reagan Administration has heretofore paid little attention to the competitive challenges facing U.S. industry. Canada's institutional impediments are not so severe as those in the United States, but Canada's poor economic performance in recent years robs Ottawa of some flexibility. The EC is hampered by slow growth, no new net employment opportunities, and institutionalized agricultural inefficiencies. Unless Europe succeeds in creating a unified market, further liberalization will prove difficult indeed. Japan is burdened by its own success. Japan's higher growth rate and lower unemployment rate provide it with greater latitude to liberalize. Other countries may emphasize that in ganging up on Japan during the negotiations. The inability or unwillingness of Japan to increase its imports of manufactured products from abroad makes it the target of every other country's complaints. Its success in exporting to the rest of the world leads to tension. As a consequence, Japanese leaders must find ways to satisfy the rest of the world without alienating their own people and interest groups.

Nonetheless, there is growing recognition throughout the industrial world that unless the trading system is updated, extended, and strengthened, it could collapse in the not-too-distant future. The price of such a collapse would be far greater than the cost of attending to the problems that beset the trading system today. Therefore, there is a commitment to begin and a belief that progress is possible, despite all the constraints.

Notes

1. For a comparison of differing U.S. and European views, see Andrew Pierre, ed., *Unemployment and Growth in Western Economies* (New York: Council on Foreign Relations, 1984).

2. OECD, *Employment Report* (Paris: OECD, 1984).

3. The joke in Europe is that Jacques Delors, the head of the European Commission, needs three cellular phones in his car when driving between EC offices in Brussels, Luxembourg, and Strasbourg.

4. Philip Hayes, "Trade and Adjustment Policies in the European Community" (London: Trade Policy Research Centre, July 1984). A simple example of increased complexity that will arise when Spain and Portugal become EC members involves translation. The number of official languages will increase from seven to nine, but the number of translations diads will jump from 42 to 72.

5. See Gardner Patterson, "The European Community as a Threat to the System," in William Cline, ed., *Trade Policy in the 1980s* (Washington: Institute for International Economics, 1983): pp. 223—42. Also see Miles Kahler, "European Protectionism in Theory and Practice," *World Politics*, vol. 37, no. 4 (July 1985), pp. 475—502. There are, however, efforts underway to relax the rule of unanimity. So far, Britain has been the main foe of such a change.

6. Secretary of State George Shultz, "National Policies and Global Prosperity," speech at Princeton University, April 11, 1985.

7. Jean-Jacques Servan-Schreiber made this point more than a decade ago in *The American Challenge* (New York: Atheneum, 1968). His warning went largely unheeded. As a result, today Europe has no effective integrated computer firm with which to compete with U.S. and Japanese firms. EC efforts in the high technology and telecommunications areas through ESPRIT and RACE are meant to assure continued European competitiveness in these areas.

8. Ernest Preeg, *Traders and Diplomats* (Washington: The Brookings Institution, 1970).

9. See Gary Saxonhouse, "The Micro- and Macroeconomics of Foreign Sales to Japan," in William Cline, ed. *Trade Policy in the 1980s* (Washington: Institute for International Economics, 1983), pp. 259—85.

10. Ambassador Brock has said that one of his worst nightmares is that Japan did everything that the United States wanted and nothing happened—the Japanese surplus continued to grow.

11. In 1984–85 over $5 billion net was being invested in the United States every month. Although efforts to internationalize the yen have been undertaken, the net effect of the effort to liberalize Japanese capital markets has been large outflows of capital into dollar-based securities which bid up the dollar.

12. Stephen Cohen and John Zysman, "The Neomercantilist Challenge to the International Trade Order," 1, *International Tax and Business Lawyer* (Summer 1983).

13. Japanese negotiators point out that the main foreign companies complaining about access to the Japanese market are not first-tier firms like IBM or AT&T with state-of-the-art technology.

14. Raymond Vernon, "International Trade Policies in the 1980s: Prospects and Problems," in *International Studies Quarterly* (December, 1982), pp. 483—510, and "Old Rules and New Players: GATT in the World Trading System," paper given at the 25th

Anniversary of the Center for International Affairs, Harvard University, March 29, 1983.

15. Furthermore, in this rapidly changing world new theories of trade based on learning curves, dynamic comparative advantage, and strategic intervention have emerged. As one prominent Japanese lobbyist put it, choosing clients is more difficult today. The world is more complicated than when only citrus, beef or baseball bats were the major issues. Today, you are not only representing clients, you are advocating theories. And you would not want to be advocating one theory one week to a member of Congress and a contradictory one the next. The European Community's frustration with Japan is indicated in its statement on the new round (see Appendix II). One of the six paragraphs of issues was devoted to the Japan problem.

16. Silicon Valley producers of semiconductors and electronic apparatus often raise this argument. The academic version of this concern is most clearly raised by John Zysman, Stephen Cohen, Laura Tyson and Michael Borrus of the Berkeley Roundtable on the International Economy.

17. Hearings on U.S.-Japanese Trade in Services before the Subcommittee on East Asia and Pacific Affairs of the Senate Foreign Relations Committee, July 18, 1985.

18. The intellectual and policy arguments for this initiative were shaped by Rodney de. C. Grey, Canada's trade negotiator during the Tokyo Round. Rodney de. C. Grey, "Traded Computer Services: An Analysis of a Proposal for Canada/U.S.A. Agreement," (Grey, Clark, Shih and Associates, for the Royal Bank of Canada, 1983).

19. Royal Commision on the Economic Union and Development Prospects for Canada, Hon. Donald MacDonald, Chairman. Report Released September 5, 1985.

20. Formal notification of the intention to negotiate bilateral agreements is required under the Trade and Tariff Act of 1984, after which Congress has 60 legislative days to disapprove of such negotiations by a majority vote in either the Senate Finance or House Ways and Means Committees. If neither committee disapproves, then any agreement negotiated is subject to "fast-track legislation" which is not amendable and which ensures Congressional action within 60 days. This authority expires on January 3, 1988. There is some ambiguity whether Congress must be notified immediately or just 60 days before the Administration begins the fast-track procedures (120 days total). In practice, however, both Finance and Ways and Means will play critical roles in the negotiations and will need to be brought into the process as soon as possible. To wait until an agreement was well along would risk disapproval by a simple majority in either Committee. Disapproval does not reject an agreement but it does bar fast-track procedures so that Congress can amend it and is not compelled to act.

21. For a well-reasoned analysis of Canadian options and perspectives on a possible Canadian-American free trade area, see Richard G. Lipsey and Murray G. Smith, *Taking the Initiative : Canada's Trade Options in a Turbulent World*, Observation No. 27, (Toronto: C.D. Howe Institute, May 1985). They argue that the status quo is unacceptable and that piecemeal approaches are likely to produce a minimum of results for a maximum of negotiating effort. They favor a comprehensive trade-liberalizing agreement aimed at providing complete coverage of all merchandise and service trade flows and eliminating substantially all trade barriers.

22. As Gilbert Winham puts it in Chapter 9, "Internal Processes," of *International Trade and the Tokyo Round Negotiations* (forthcoming, Princeton University Press, 1986), "one sees the tendency of large external negotiations to expose the building blocks of which nations are constituted."

Six

The Developing Countries

Economic interests in the developing world diverge even more than the economic interests among industrial countries. For reasons of strategy and solidarity, however, developing countries usually maintain a united front when dealing with the industrial world on economic issues. In practice, this means that the largest, most influential developing countries dominate the stage with regard to planned trade negotiations. Brazil, India, Argentina, Indonesia, and a few other middle-level powers tend to be the most influential. Mexico and Saudi Arabia would normally play key roles, but are less important in this context because neither is a member of GATT. Whether these countries reflect the true interests of rapidly developing smaller countries such as Singapore, Malaysia, Taiwan, or Hong Kong, or of China, the OPEC countries, Egypt, Pakistan, or the poorest, least developed countries is less clear.

Even though they disagree with India and Brazil on critical topics, many smaller countries have not been willing thus far to rock the boat and threaten the LDC united front. So long as LDCs group themselves as a bloc, the industrial countries treat them as one. This chapter first looks at what trade concessions the developing countries hope to gain from the industrial world, and vice versa. The second section examines how LDC interests differ. The third section considers the positions of key countries or groups and assesses their special circumstances; the primary goals of each group in the coming negotiations are considered.

The LDCs as a Bloc

Whether as colonies or independent states, developing countries believe they have consistently lost out economically to industrial countries. To remedy their backward situation, leaders of third world countries decided to work together as a bloc. On a political basis, developing countries began to cooperate at the first meeting of the "nonaligned countries" at Bandung, Indonesia in 1954. African and Asian leaders dominated this group. Ten years later, under the leadership of Latin American technocrats, developing countries formed a cohesive bloc, the Group of 77, to work for LDC economic interests in the U.N. Conference on Trade and Development (UNCTAD) and in other international settings. In 1973 at the Algiers summit of the nonaligned, top-level political leaders for the first time decided to use their political clout and cohesion to achieve economic ends. The success of the OPEC countries in quadrupling oil prices in 1973—74 acted as an incentive to all LDCs to try to cooperate when dealing with industrial countries.[1]

Industrial countries complain that the bloc system has politicized economic and social deliberations and that it does not really help the interests of most developing countries. They note that the developing countries have opposed reciprocity and most-favored-nation treatment under the GATT. As a consequence, LDCs and particularly the least developed countries have benefited much less from the various multilateral trade rounds than have the major industrial-country participants. LDCs continue to face higher tariffs in industrial countries on products of particular interest to them than on the products of other industrial countries. Leaders from developing countries retort that their strength is in numbers and their unity is the only leverage they have in bargaining with the industrial countries. In the past, the United Nations and its satellite organizations were dominated by East-West bargaining from which the developing world gained little. Today, North-South discussions dominate the international economic scene. Therefore, the LDCs are loathe to yield the only significant bargaining advantage they possess—their unity and bloc voting.

As a group, developing countries do not accept the underlying premise of the GATT that free trade is the best way to promote domestic growth and development. A quarter-century ago most LDCs' trade policies were heavily biased in favor of import substitution and against exports. In the 1960s Singapore, South Korea and Taiwan were the first to turn away from import-substitution policies and to promote manufactured exports. Today, manufactured products account for 90 percent of South Korea's exports, 50 percent or more of exports from India, Singapore, Taiwan and Hong Kong; and between 20 and 40 percent of those from Latin America and second-tier Asian NICs. Indeed, studies for the National Bureau for Economic Research found a close correlation between manufactured

exports and growth.[2] Still, many LDCs do not believe that liberalization as advocated by industrial countries is in their best interests.
They try to promote exports and limit imports. LDCs are happy to
claim the benefits derived from unconditional most-favored-nation
treatment, but they insist on their right to intervene in their own
economies and to discriminate against imports from abroad.

Ever since the beginning of GATT, debates have raged over the
role of the LDCs in the trading system. The LDCs argued that
"equal treatment of unequals is unjust." GATT was a "rich man's
club" from which they benefited little. They felt the system should
be tilted in their favor, that they should be given preferential treatment. The first several rounds of trade negotiations contributed to
this impression because in tariff negotiations the countries with the
largest volume of trade dominate. They are seeking the most and
they have much more to give in terms of market access.

Just as UNCTAD was being formed in 1964, GATT adopted Part
IV of the Agreement to deal with the problems of the developing
countries. Part IV comprises three Articles which were approved by
the Contracting Parties in November 1964 and which went into
effect in 1966. These articles allowed developing countries not to
extend reciprocal concessions to the industrial countries in tariff
negotiations. Part IV also made it easier for LDCs to claim an exception from GATT Articles for policies which contribute to their development.

Preferential treatment was not resolved by Part IV but was pur-
sued further at UNCTAD and eventually a ten-year GATT waiver
(from MFN) was granted in 1971. The U.S. and other countries' generalized system of preference (GSP) programs fell under this waiver.
Many observers felt that as a result the legal relationship between
industrial and developing countries based upon the GATT code fell
apart. Industrial countries came to view LDCs as nonpaying participants which no longer had a right to make claims on the system.[3]
The 1973 Ministerial declaration which launched the Tokyo Round
stressed the need to give "special and differential" treatment to the
developing countries in the nontariff negotiations. At the close of
the Tokyo Round in 1979, special and differential treatment was
legitimized through an "enabling clause" which allowed, but did
not require, contracting parties to give preferential treatment to
developing countries despite the MFN requirement of Article I of
the GATT. In return, the developing countries accepted a graduation
concept by which their ability to make concessions "would improve

with the progressive development of their economies."[4] The LDCs got what they wanted, but in the process a "tiered" GATT emerged and the possibility of more political pressure for graduation increased.[5]

In short, the trend in the trading system has been to treat the developing countries as exceptions and to accord them special status. But this proved a two-edged sword. Because the LDCs are not required in negotiations to give reciprocity to the industrial countries, they got little in return. In practice, special treatment effectively discourages both sides from reducing trade barriers. The LDCs' opposition to reciprocity was perhaps rational when they were minor players in the trading system, unconditional MFN was abided by, and tariff cuts were the major issue. But today, unconditional MFN is less important, and the debt crisis demonstrated that LDCs have become central players.

Since the onset of the debt crisis in mid-1982, many LDCs, particularly those in Latin America that were forced to adopt austerity programs to reorient their economies and meet their external obligations, have cut back dramatically on imports and become more protectionist. U.S. exports to Latin America fell by $14 billion in two years. Some in these countries believe that their problems were caused by letting in too much foreign capital and too many imports. Furthermore, they insist that if LDCs gave in to the demands for industrial countries for more open markets, the result would be renewed domestic economic disruption and another bout of debt crisis.[6]

LDC goals in new negotiations can be put into four categories. First, developing countries want to continue to receive special and differential treatment from industrial countries. They do not want to graduate from LDC status. They want to hold on to their ability to obtain derogations from GATT rules to promote infant industries and to subsidize manufactured exports. They also will try to avoid binding their tariffs and agreeing to full reciprocity in terms of their GATT obligations.

Second, LDCs want industrial countries to grant them more market access for their exports. The developing countries complain that tariffs in industrial countries remain on average higher on their exports than on products exported from other industrial countries. Furthermore, effective protection in industrial countries is also biased against LDCs because tariffs are generally higher on processed products than on raw materials (escalating or cascading tariffs, depending on which way you look at them).[7] Specifically, LDCs want more access for their textiles, apparel, footwear, and steel throughout the industrial world. They seek the elimination of quantitative restrictions and nontariff barriers against their agricultural and tropical products and they want industrial countries to lift their GATT-inconsistent protective measures.

Commodities are a particular priority of the LDCs. Trade in primary commodities such as cocoa, sugar, rubber, and tin is extremely volatile, particularly prices, making planning difficult for producers and consumers. Projections suggest that the chances for major price advances from the already depressed 1985 levels are not great. If anything the problems of some commodities will get worse as new materials (e.g., fiber optics, ceramics) become available as substitutes. Several commodity agreements have tried, with limited success, to use buffer stocks of commodity reserves to stabilize prices, but surpluses have often arisen, depressing prices. For example, although the multilateral agreement for rubber has functioned quite well, the agreement has failed to hold prices above the specified floor level, and the sugar agreement collapsed in 1984 when the largest sugar producer, the EC, refused to agree to terms acceptable to the other major producers.[8]

The United States would like to see greater structural adaptation of the commodity-producing economies. The LDCs counter with arguments for assured higher prices and some form of "safety net" to protect their foreign earnings, guarantee a predictable flow of foreign exchange earnings, and allow them to service their international debts. They seek adequate sources of compensatory financing to extend product coverage to more commodities and to cover commodity exports going to any destination. As with agriculture, we expect a great deal of acrimony and debate about commodities and tropical products to emerge from new trade talks, but we do not believe that fundamental progress is likely anytime soon.

Third, LDCs want the industrial countries to adhere to GATT disciplines, to avoid dicriminatory trade practices, and to stop using domestic unfair trade laws to limit their exports. The LDCs realize that Japanese imports of their manufactured products have fallen in relative terms. Europe and the United States are also putting more and more roadblocks in the way of their exports. They are particularly frustrated in that when they develop manufactured products that are competitive in industrial countries, they are often hit with quantitative restrictions, tariffs, and nontariff barriers which prevent them from using those few advantages they possess to gain more than a small foothold. They also want the industrial countries to stop taking illegal safeguard actions that often take the form of discriminatory, bilateral circumventions which hit them directly or indirectly through trade diversion. The LDCs would also like to see industrial countries cut their use of countervailing and anti-dumping duties against their exports and abstain from challenging their export subsidies under the subsidy code.

Fourth, the LDCs want to limit the discussion and progress on investment and services issues. LDCs note that although they are constantly pressured to permit freer flows of capital into their countries, industrial countries rule out of hand the possibility of a freer flow of labor from developing to industrial countries. In a well-reasoned critique of the trading system and U.S. initiatives at the 1982 Ministerial Meeting, Carlos Diaz-Alejandro and Gerald Helleiner argued that a broad reform agenda should include a "GATT for immigration" as well as a "GATT for investment".[9] At the Ministerial, the Indian trade minister asked whether services also included labor services and, if so, how immigration would be dealt with. Developing country leaders often distinguish between high-technology and labor-intensive services. The industrial countries, they claim, only want to discuss high-technology services.

From an industrial-country perspective, the initial demands of the LDCs amount to asking for greater access to developed country markets while keeping their own markets closed. At the same time, the LDCs want the industrial world to conform to the GATT when it benefits the cause of their development, but they do not want to submit to GATT discipline that might constrain their flexibility to deal with their current domestic economic problems and their longer-term development plans.

Not surprisingly, the industrial world has a radically different agenda of issues which it wants considered.

Industrial countries believe that they gave more to the LDCs than they got in return in past trade negotiations. This was acceptable because the LDCs needed help, but also because North-South trade as a proportion of total world trade was not very important. Now that LDCs play a larger role in world trade, the industrial countries seek concessions in five main areas: acceptance of GATT discipline, reduction of protectionist barriers to imports, elimination of certain export practices, acceptance of the principle of graduation, and reform of practices on foreign investment.

Although they recognize that the current difficult economic situation makes full-scale liberalization of LDC import barriers impractical, the industrial countries' first objective is to get the LDCs to accept in principle their responsibilities within an interdependent trading system. Beyond limited compliance with national treatment and nondiscrimination obligations, industrial countries complain that LDCs have not accepted their full share of obligations under the GATT. Even though the LDCs benefit from the application of most-favored-nation treatment by the industrial world, they continue to discriminate against industrial-country exporters. In particular, the industrial countries want the LDCs to accept rules that would define when they might derogate from their GATT obligations because of balance-of-payments problems and impose predictability and time limits on their ability to escape from their obligations. The industrial world wants LDC commitments that they will deal with reciprocity and begin to bind their tariffs.

Second, the industrial countries want more access to developing country markets. At the very least, they want the rules restricting their sales to LDCs to be rationalized, liberalized, and made more transparent. The industrial countries stress that these are goals toward which to work; there is no expectation that changes will take place overnight. With regard to tariffs and barriers at the border, industrial countries seek reduction and possibly realignments of the extremely high tariffs that LDCs impose and also the easing of restrictions that ban the importation of luxury items in many LDCs.

The industrial countries have a number of other objectives that would make it easier for them to sell to LDCs. Industrial countries would like the LDCs to agree to limit the level and duration of their support for infant industries, to open up government procurement to foreign producers, to relax and make more transparent the barriers hampering trade in services, and eventually to eliminate discretionary licensing policies.

Third, LDCs are being pressured to eliminate or at least reduce many of their current export subsidies. In addition, the LDCs can expect to come under increasing pressure to stop producing and exporting counterfeit goods and to complete negotiations on the counterfeit code begun during the Tokyo Round. A related item involves intellectual property. The United States and Europe are growing more and more insistent that LDCs, particularly such NICs as Singapore, Hong Kong, Taiwan, and South Korea, respect the intellectual property of western companies and pay appropriate licensing fees and royalties.

Fourth, industrial countries want the richer LDCs to accept the principle of graduation and negotiate measures, targets, and time schedules which would determine when, in what sectors, and at what pace the NICs would accept full trade and financial obligations and discipline. The industrial countries point out that they are not asking NICs, such as Brazil and Argentina, to give up benefits until their economies are back on track. In addition, their advantages might be retained in sectors that are not yet competitive. Special and differential treatment could, in theory, be granted in new sectors, including services and high-technology products. Graduation also would make poorer LDCs more competitive because some new for- eign investment and export sales that go to the richer NICs might be diverted to them. To date, however, the NICs have bitterly opposed graduation, regardless of how well their economies are performing. The least developed countries have so far not pushed them to gradu- ate. They do not want to risk splitting the LDC bloc and diminishing its bargaining leverage.

In this regard, it is of some note that the recently released GATT Wisemen's report criticized preferential treatment, stating that it has been of limited value and arguing that greater emphasis should be put on integrating the LDCs more fully into the trading system. If the new recommendations gain wide acceptance, it would be a departure from the trend in trade policy that has been in force since the enactment of Part IV of the GATT in 1964.[10]

Fifth, the corporate community continues to press the develop- ing countries to liberalize their treatment of foreign investment. In particular, industrial countries' multinational companies want their governments to pressure LDCs to guarantee rights of establish- ment, eliminate performance requirements, ease ownership restraints, guarantee that profits and dividends can be remitted to headquarters, and agree to the international arbitration of invest- ment disputes. LDCs counter that these are investment issues and should not be discussed under the auspices of GATT negotiations.

How Do LDC Interests Differ?

Two overlapping economic divisions among LDC ranks help clarify possible LDC divisions during future trade negotiations. First, LDC growth records and prospects differ. The richest developing countries grew extremely rapidly during the 1970s, but their expansion came to an abrupt halt in the early 1980s. During the 1970s, for example, NICs' share in OECD imports of manufactured products rose from 4.3 to 8.9 percent. At the same time, the poorest developing countries lost, and continue to lose, ground. The gap between the NICs and the industrial world may actually be narrowing on some criteria. The gap between the NICs and the least developed countries is widening alarmingly. Table 6.1 compares the economic performance of the OECD countries and selected developing countries as measured by per capita GNP and real growth rates over the period 1960—82. Note that several NICs' per capita GNP now exceeds some OECD countries and that they have consistently had higher growth rates. On the other hand, the poorest countries in Africa are far behind and barely growing at all.

Although the richer developing countries, including those in OPEC, Latin American countries, and Asian NICs, attracted significant investment from industrial countries and were able to borrow large sums of money from money-center banks in the 1970s, the least developed countries remained, for the most part, dependent on bilateral and multilateral aid and loans. The variable performance of the LDCs has persuaded industrial countries that they should not all be treated the same—thus the attention to graduation.

A second difference among developing countries centers on the relative debt problems of different countries, which depend upon both the volume of borrowing and the volume of exports. As official lending declined at the end of the 1960s, Western banks began lending more to the richer, relatively credit-worthy developing countries. These borrowers believed that they would be less dependent if they borrowed money and developed their own domestic industries than if they allowed foreign multinational companies to dominate their domestic economies. The process was accelerated after the 1973—74 oil crisis left banks holding billions of petrodollars that they needed to lend. Whether banks overlent or borrowers overborrowed matters less than the resulting debt problems of the early 1980s.

When recession struck in the early 1980s and Mexico suddenly discovered it was unable to service its debt, a crisis broke in August 1982. Four groups of debtor countries can be distinguished.[11]

(1) A few Arab OPEC members are still net creditors. Other Arab/OPEC countries continue to be credit-worthy, but slowed their borrowing when oil income fell.

TABLE 6.1

Per Capita Income and Real Growth, Selected Countries

	Per Capita GNP (U.S. dollars) 1982	Average Real Growth (% per annum) 1960-82
OECD Countries		
Australia	11,140	2.4
Austria	9,880	3.9
Belgium	10,760	3.6
Canada	11,320	3.1
Denmark	12,470	2.5
Finland	10,870	3.6
France	11,680	3.7
Greece	4,290	5.2
Iceland	12,150	3.2
Ireland	5,150	2.9
Italy	6,840	3.4
Japan	10,080	6.1
Netherlands	10,930	2.9
New Zealand	7,920	1.5
Norway	14,280	3.4
Portugal	2,450	4.8
Spain	5,430	4.0
Sweden	14,040	2.4
Switzerland	17,010	1.9
Turkey	1,370	3.4
United Kingdom	9,660	2.0
United States	13,160	2.2
Germany (Fed. Rep.)	12,460	3.1
Yugoslavia	2,800	4.9
Developing Countries		
All Developing Countries	787	3.1
Hong Kong	5,340	7.0
Korea (Rep. of)	1,910	6.6
Singapore	5,910	7.4
Taiwan	2,540	NA
Brazil	2,240	4.8
Mexico	2,270	3.7
China	310	5.0
Low-Income Africa	246	0.5

Source: Overseas Development Council, *U.S. Foreign Policy and the Third World: Agenda 1985-86*, Table E-1.

(2) At the other extreme were the problem debtors. Mexico, Brazil, and Argentina became the focus of international efforts to make sure that their problems were resolved because if they did not service their debts, the entire financial system could be in jeopardy. Smaller Latin American countries, such as Peru and Chile, the Philippines, as well as Zaire and Poland also found themselves in over their heads. They received somewhat less publicity and attention, however, because the numbers were smaller and because the banks and the financial system would not be shaken if only one or two of them failed to repay its debts. Still these countries were troublesome because there was fear of a domino default. At one point in mid-1983, all Latin American countries, except Colombia and Paraguay, were in arrears on their debt-servicing to their foreign creditors.

(3) High-debt LDCs without major servicing problems, mainly the Asian NICs, built up significant foreign external debt, but continued to service their obligations from their export earnings. Although such countries as South Korea worry that they may come to be viewed as not credit-worthy, banks, after some initial assessment-taking, continued to lend to these export-oriented NICs.

(4) Finally, except for Zaire, most of the least developed countries were not severely hurt by the private debt problems because they had never been able to borrow significant amounts of medium- and long-term funds from the banks. Even India and Pakistan, which had tapped private markets, remained much more dependent on official aid and borrowing. At the time of the crisis, China had little external debt. (However, countries such as India and Bangladesh as well as many African nations are experiencing growing difficulty in repaying their World Bank and IMF loans.)

If countries are arrayed according to export performance, a similar pattern emerges. The richer OPEC countries, particularly those without serious population pressures, are mainly dependent on petroleum exports for export earnings. They are trying to develop their domestic infrastructure and industry. Because petroleum and natural gas products are dealt with outside the GATT system, these countries will not be major players in the coming negotiations.

The least developed countries also are most concerned with only a few narrow issues. They want access for their commodity exports at high, stable prices. They have few manufactured products to sell to industrial countries, and therefore are not worried about graduating or about high-technology exports.

In contrast, most high-debt LDCs have been less successful exporters and more restrictive on imports than the Asian NICs. The Asian NICs have survived the debt rollercoaster because they continue to export their goods to the industrial countries. Significantly, the Asian NICs recognize their success under the GATT system and may be willing to support and strengthen the system even if this threatens to undermine LDC solidarity. They are pragmatists. If they must yield on counterfeiting and intellectual property issues and even graduation to get what they want, they will do so. High-debt Latin Americans remain preoccupied with finance and debt issues.

The success of the Asian NICs has been extraordinary as several of them have ascended to the top of the list of exporting countries. Table 6.2 compares the top twenty exporting and importing countries in 1973 and 1984. Note that six new countries appear on the list of exporters in 1984: Taiwan, South Korea, Hong Kong, China, Mexico and Singapore. Export expansion in Australia, Poland, Denmark, Iran, Czechoslovakia, and East Germany was not sufficient to keep them among the top twenty even though their growth rates of exports ranged from 6–11 percent annually. Taiwan and South Korea have also moved ahead of traditional exporters Sweden and Switzerland. Their export performance reinforces the point that the NICs should be required to graduate into the ranks of the industrial countries.

Another important conclusion, however, can be drawn from the change in the list of the twenty largest importers between 1973 and 1984. South Korea, Singapore, Hong Kong, China, Taiwan and Saudi Arabia are now among the top importers. Poland, Denmark, Austria, Brazil, Norway, and East Germany are no longer among the top twenty importers.[12] Not only have the Asian NICs and China demonstrated export competitiveness but they are now among the largest markets. The industrial countries have a stake in getting these dynamic countries to the bargaining table. For example, 40 percent of U.S. exports now go to the developing world. Developing countries can no longer be ignored as competitors or as markets.

Constraints on Specific Countries and Groups of Countries

From the point of view of industrial countries, the ability and willingness of the NICs to participate fully in new trade talks is constrained by three main policy stances. First, most LDCs actively

TABLE 6.2 Leading Exporters and Importers in World Merchandise Trade in 1984 (and compared with 1973)

Exports

Rank 1984	Rank 1973	Area	Percentage share in the value of world exports 1984	Percentage share in the value of world exports 1973
1	1	United States	11.4	12.2
2	2	Germany (Fed. Rep.)	8.9	11.7
3	3	Japan	8.9	6.4
4	4	France	4.9	6.3
5	5	United Kingdom	4.9	5.3
6	10	USSR	4.8	3.7
7	6	Canada	4.4	4.4
8	9	Italy	3.8	3.9
9	7	Netherlands	3.4	4.2
10	8	Belgium-Luxembourg	2.7	3.9
11	14	Saudi Arabia	2.1	1.6
12	27	Taiwan	1.6	0.8
13	11	Sweden	1.5	2.1
14	35	Korea (Rep. of)	1.5	0.6
15	24	Hong Kong	1.5	0.9
16	19	Brazil	1.4	1.1
17	12	Switzerland	1.3	1.7
18	21	China	1.3	1.0
19	41	Mexico	1.3	0.4
20	23	Singapore	1.3	0.6
		Total of above	72.9	73.5
		World trade	100.0	100.0

Imports

Rank 1984	Rank 1973	Area	Percentage share in the value of world imports 1984	Percentage share in the value of world imports 1973
1	1	United States	17.1	11.6
2	2	Germany (Fed. Rep.)	7.6	9.2
3	4	Japan	6.7	6.5
4	3	United Kingdom	5.3	6.6
5	5	France	5.2	6.3
6	6	Italy	4.1	4.7
7	10	USSR	4.0	3.6
8	8	Canada	3.8	3.9
9	7	Netherlands	3.1	4.1
10	9	Belgium-Luxembourg	2.7	3.7
11	47	Saudi Arabia	1.7	0.3
12	29	Korea (Rep. of)	1.5	0.7
13	11	Switzerland	1.5	2.0
14	13	Spain	1.4	1.6
15	24	Singapore	1.4	0.9
16	22	Hong Kong	1.4	1.0
17	19	Australia	1.3	1.2
18	12	Sweden	1.3	1.8
19	23	China	1.3	0.9
20	31	Taiwan	1.1	0.6
		Total of above	73.5	72.2
		World trade	100.0	100.0

Source: GATT, Prospects for International Trade, Press Release 1374, September 26, 1985.

work to promote exports and simultaneously erect barriers to limit imports. This is a long-standing policy stance, but it was reinforced and perpetuated by the oil crisis of the 1970s and the debt problems of the early 1980s. Second, most LDCs are more comfortable negotiating bilateral arrangements with their key trading partners than with participating actively in multilateral discussions. This bilateral tendency reinforces restrictions on trade. Third, the NICs' subordination of their individual interests to group discipline leads to inaction on GATT issues and sometimes bloc confrontations. It is harder to find agreement through the development of cross-cutting cleavages when LDCs (like the European Community) must first develop consensus around the lowest common denominator.[13] Specific constraints on the key groups of LDCs are considered below.

High-Debt LDCs

The chief victims of the debt crises of the early 1980s are constrained from active participation in new trade talks by their need to pay primary attention to their debt and internal economic position. They would prefer to work their way through their austerity programs before even considering opening up their markets to foreign imports. To the extent that the Latin debtors have rebounded, their success came in large part from cutting imports while continuing to export. Accordingly, they are unwilling to talk of graduation and liberalization at present.

At the same time, it is widely recognized that there is an important linkage between trade and debt.[14] Both industrial and developing countries have a strong incentive to continue to encourage LDC exports. Market access is critical for future LDC recovery and growth but also is absolutely necessary to prevent the recurrence of severe debt crises. Beyond the short run, import restrictions by debtor countries cannot be an enduring solution. The severe import cuts by debtor countries are provoking simultaneous surges in inflation and steep declines in output. As domestic austerity measures are undertaken to control inflation, output will drop still further. Indeed, even if import cuts did not hurt the debtors' trading partners, the ultimate prosperity of the debtors depends largely on continued imports. Without them, growth is far less likely.

The only way in which debtor nations will be able to resolve their financial problems while resuming growth is if they are able to increase their exports. Yet here a crucial variable emerges: what if problem debtors cannot gain needed access to markets of industrial countries? This might happen if the Latin debtors refuse to discuss eventual graduation and will not commit themselves to observing greater discipline in the future.

This possibility raises the specter of a mutually reinforcing debt/trade crisis. A loss of confidence by lenders creates a balance-of-payments crunch for high-debt LDCs. Attempting to cope with the shortfall, the LDCs try to push their exports as much as possible. The export drive of LDCs increases pressure on politically sensitive labor-intensive industries in industrial countries. These industries seek and receive protection. Bankers, seeing that debtors are having difficulty in increasing their exports, become even less willing to lend. With this increased balance-of-payments pressure debtors make further efforts to promote exports. The cycle begins again.[15]

Before long, the process could lead to both a moratorium or repudiation of debt and a disruption of North-South trade. Therefore, it is critical that industrial and developing countries walk a tightrope which promotes trade in both directions without provoking another round of debt problems. Timing will be critical.

Mexico

A special case among the high-debt LDCs is Mexico. It is the third largest trading partner of the United States and a leader of the developing world. In early 1980, after prolonged negotiations, the Lopez Portillo government decided against becoming a contracting party to the GATT. The situation was and remains so politicized that there is little prospect that Mexico will join GATT any time soon. Nonetheless, significant bureaucratic players within the Mexican government favored becoming part of GATT and still would like to participate in some way in continuing trade negotiations. The leading GATT sympathizers in Mexico seem to be the finance ministry and the central bank, which viewed GATT membership as leverage to improve Mexico's bargaining position on international financial and debt issues. President de la Madrid, as a Cabinet member in 1980, voted for Mexico accepting GATT membership. Although it seems probable that Mexico may cooperate on certain parts of the negotiations preceding and during a new round, including services, it will not play a leading role and is less likely to gain the benefits of any concessions made in these trade talks than in previous rounds.

Asian NICs

The Asian NICs can be grouped in three categories. The first tier consists of the "Gang of Four" (Hong Kong, South Korea, Singapore, and Taiwan) all of which have shown tremendous growth linked with active export industries. In general, these countries have also been relatively more open to foreign imports than other LDCs. Second-tier Asian NICs include Malaysia, Thailand, and the Philippines (which is also a high-debt LDC). A third tier includes India, Pakistan, and Indonesia.

The "Gang of Four" are probably more willing to participate in new trade talks than any other LDCs. They gained under the old system; they believe their continued growth and increased access to industrial-country markets depends on strengthening the system. Malaysia and Thailand have the same general interests and seem willing to enter into new trade talks as well.

In contrast, India (along with Brazil) has been the most outspoken opponent of a new trade round generally, and of new issues such as services in particular. India, unlike almost all the other NICs, never turned away from import-substitution policies. Like Brazil, India has a much smaller external sector than the other NICs. Although its exports of manufactured goods increased by about 10 percent annually during the 1970s, its industry is less efficient than many of its NIC competitors. But, it seems that Rajiv Gandhi is beginning to change some key domestic economic policies, and internal changes are underway at the highest levels of the bureaucracy. Eventually international policies may also change, particularly since key Indian economists and the World Bank agree that Indian exports must grow at close to 7 percent if India's overall economy is to grow at the 5 percent level India seeks.

The major question concerning the Asian NICs is whether the "Gang of Four" and a few others might be willing to enter into serious talks with industrial countries. Certainly, their bargaining leverage is greater than ever before. In a world of slow growth, they are the fastest growing markets. These countries have also realized that their continued success depends upon their ability to export. Their export-led growth has convinced them that maintenance of the trading system is more important than ever before. South Korea, for example, is actively exploring the possibility of joining the OECD. (Its GNP per capita is roughly 1.5 times as great as Turkey's, which is a member!) The active participation of these dynamic countries is critical. Consider how much further they could advance during a decade of negotiations. For everyone's benefit, they must be involved from the outset in the bargaining process.

At the Stockholm meeting of trade ministers in June 1985, South Korea and other countries including Uruguay and the Philippines, clearly indicated their willingness to break with the LDC bloc under some circumstances. In the event that India and Brazil continue to block progress on multilateral negotiations, at least some LDCs might break ranks to get discussions going. Once talks begin, individual NICs probably will work for those narrow agreements and arrangements that most interest them, but which do not threaten bloc solidarity.

China

China, paradoxically, is neither and both an Asian NIC and a least developed country. It could, however, be a key player in new trade talks. Chinese imports will increase significantly as China industrializes during the rest of the century and beyond. Japanese, European, American, Asian NIC, and even Indian companies compete to sell plants and technologically advanced equipment in the Chinese market. China is likely to increase its foreign debt. But to pay for the flood of imports, China must expand its exports.

China is not now a member of the GATT, but it sought and received observer status in 1984. The United States granted it most-favored-nation status in 1982. China so far has not sought to play a major role in Third World economic deliberations and is not a member of the Group of 77 bloc of LDCs. Nevertheless, its potential clout in international markets make it a wild card in the coming negotiations. To the extent that China cooperates in new talks, it will reap growth benefits even if it submits to some discipline within the GATT.

The industrial countries might give China, the new and obviously significant player, important short-term benefits in exchange for Chinese willingness to begin to integrate itself into the trading system. China will extract whatever concessions it can. At the same time, China will almost certainly support third-world positions with regard to textiles and agriculture and, more generally, with regard to market access both as a way to convey its support for LDCs and because it stands to benefit as well. Nor does China have any incentive to diverge from the third world on services. It does seem, however, that China could serve as a moderating force in new negotiations. To the extent that it wishes to cooperate with the industrial countries, China may pull some LDCs along. At the same time, China will add weight to LDC demands for concessions in key areas such as textiles, steel, market access, and agriculture. On the other hand, there is also a discernible hesitancy: some LDCs are concerned about China because of its great export potential. They fear that the whale might leap into the swimming pool.

The Least Developed Countries

The least favored nations have much to gain from new trade talks and will be asked to give almost nothing. These poorest countries generally resist GATT discipline and are permitted to do what they please. Population growth has exceeded economic growth, and their relative welfare has suffered. Yet, the poorest LDCs have supported the leading, richer, LDC procrastinators out of solidarity. Significantly, those few countries (e.g., the Ivory Coast and Zimbabwe), which have downplayed rhetoric, have tried to encourage foreign investment, have patterned their policies more on those of the Asian NICs than of India or the Latin American countries, and have been more successful in their development programs. Possibly, these countries would benefit most if they worked for greater discipline in the GATT and stopped complaining about the unfairness of the existing rules.

If their richer bloc partners could be encouraged to graduate, more opportunities would be left to the rest. The least developed countries are also concerned with the access of tropical products to OECD markets and could progress if they gained a larger share of textile quotas in the industrial world. The greatest resource these countries have is their cheap labor; but population is also their greatest problem. Industrial countries will not throw open their borders to migration, but some concessions on trade are possible which would let poorer countries use their labor advantages.

For years the least developed countries have argued that the system was rigged against their interests and that they should be compensated both with new rules that favored them and with generous measures that redistributed Northern wealth to the South. The New International Economic Order may have gotten LDC issues on the agenda and increased LDC political influence, but it did not improve LDC growth and development. The least developed countries will consequently have to decide whether political power through confrontation or economic growth through cooperation is in their best interest.[16] Global redistribution of wealth is not, however, in the cards. Increasingly, it looks as though the least developed countries may actually have harmed their development prospects by protecting their markets. Now they must consider whether greater cooperation with the industrial countries is in their interest.

The poorest of the least developed in Africa, however, have little prospect of immediate gains from trade liberalization, particularly since it will not come for years. Expanded concessional assistance through the World Bank is essential. Here as on trade issues United States leadership is key. With 25 percent of World Bank quotas, U.S. positions determine what the increase in World Bank resources will be. By keeping contributions down to $2.25 billion (over 3 years), the United States cut the size of the most recent replenishment down to $9 billion rather than the $12 billion the other major countries were willing to go along with. The United States had also been unwilling to go along with a special facility for Africa, but now there are some signs that it may reverse its position on concessional aid for Africa and on World Bank resources. Nonetheless, for the forseeable future, Africa, and particularly sub-Saharan Africa, will have to depend upon concessional assistance. Trade liberalization and greater discipline will benefit those countries but only over the longer term.

Oil Producing Countries

As a group, the OPEC countries are unlikely to play a role in the coming trade talks. OPEC countries outside the Middle East, such as Nigeria and Indonesia, are plagued by population pressures and are oriented more by their debt and development policies than by oil. Iran, Iraq and Libya are at war with the world and with each other. Saudi Arabia, Venezuela, and Mexico are not members of the GATT. Most important, the oil and natural gas trade is not now (nor has it ever been) covered under the GATT. (Coal and nuclear power are not covered either.) By value, the energy trade is the largest component of world trade; but energy, and hence OPEC, will not take center stage in future negotiations. Although market forces intervened to drive down oil prices from the high level to which OPEC, and to some extent the oil companies, drove them, energy is and will remain a managed market. Neither the oil companies nor the oil producers have any interest in bringing energy into the GATT.

***

The demands of the LDCs are largely the mirror image of what the industrial countries want. This suggests that bargains should be possible. But the bargains face serious political obstacles: international political obstacles along North-South ideological lines, and domestic political obstacles in both LDCs and industrial countries. Labor-adjustment problems create domestic political obstacles in the industrial countries. Nationalism, infant-industry aspirations, and unemployment (and underemployment) create domestic political obstacles in LDCs.

North-South issues should not be the central focus of the new round. These issues will not engage the North, where they are political non-starters. Although the debt crisis demonstrated the central significance of the developing world and the necessity that those countries maintain and increase exports, the problems afflicting the trading system are global. To achieve significant progress on trade, specific issues need to cut across industrial and developing countries.

The international political obstacles could be overcome if some of the Asian NICs split off from the LDC bloc. Overcoming domestic political obstacles, in the LDCs as elsewhere, will depend upon strong support from private interests with a stake in expanding trade. The economic success of the outward-looking Asian NICs is an example for other LDCs seeking to redefine their trade policies.

Notes

1. See Karl Sauvant, *The Group of 77: Evolution, Structure and Organization* (New York: Oceana Press, 1981); Gerald Helleiner, ed. *International Economic Disorder: Essays on North-South Relations* (Toronto: University of Toronto Press, 1981); and Jeffrey Hart, *The New International Order* (New York: Macmillan, 1983).

2. See Anne O. Krueger, *Foreign Trade Regimes and Economic Development: Liberalization Attempts and Consequences* (Cambridge: Ballinger, 1978), and Jagdish N. Bhagwati, *Foreign Trade Regimes and Economic Development: Anatomy and Consequences of Exchange Control Regimes* (Cambridge: Ballinger, 1978).

3. See, for example, Robert Hudec, *The GATT Legal System and World Trade Diplomacy* (New York: Praeger, 1975), p. 211.

4. *Agreements Relating to the Framework for the Conduct of International Trade* (Geneva: GATT, 1979).

5. Graduation is an emotive word which tends to polarize discussions. It is used here as shorthand. A more constructive approach would be talk about contributions that each country can make. The system is not working well. There should be a reciprocity of interest in improving it. In that concern all have contributions to make. Instead of graduation, then, we could speak of incorporation into a different, better functioning system.

6. Imagine the case of Brazil. If it lowered its barriers against imports of technologically sophisticated products and services, its imports would increase. On the other hand,

from Brazil's perspective, that would force it to cut back imports in other areas to maintain any semblance of balance-of-payments discipline. Brazil chooses to select what it will limit directly and not to impose an overall limit on total value of goods and services that may be imported in any year.

7. Rudiger Dornbusch and Jeffrey Frankel, "Macroeconomics and Protection," University of Michigan Conference on U.S. Trade Policies in a Changing World Economy, March 28-29, 1985. They demonstrated that tariffs on finished manufactures in the industrial countries were about four times higher than tariffs on raw materials.

8. John D.A. Cuddy, "Commodity Trade," in Ernest H. Preeg, ed., *Hard Bargaining Ahead: U.S. Trade Policy and Developing Countries* (New Brunswick, N.J.: Transaction Books, for the Overseas Development Council, 1985), pp. 117—33.

9. "Handmaiden in Distress: World Trade in the 1980s" (Washington: Overseas Development Council, September 1982).

10. *Trade Policies for a Better Future: Proposals for Action*, GATT, March 1985. The previous GATT Wisemen's report, *Trends in World Trade* (1958), Gottfried Haberler, chairman, gave a big push to the drive toward preferential treatment. Over 25 years later, another group of seven distinguished individuals, including three from developing countries, found it to have been misguided. In the words of the new report, "'special and differential' treatment has been of limited value. Developing countries are not required in negotiations to give reciprocity to developed countries. In practice, this effectively discourages both sides from reducing trade barriers. Developing countries have allowed themselves to be distracted by the idea of preferences. They have done so at the cost of overlooking their fundamental interest in a nondiscriminatory trading system. . . . Far greater emphasis should be placed on integrating them (developing countries) more fully into the trading system." (p. 44)

11. Jonathan Aronson, "Muddling Through the Debt Decade," in W. Ladd Hollist and F. LaMond Tullis, eds., *An International Political Economy*, International Political Yearbook, vol. 1 (Boulder: Westview Press, 1985), pp. 127—51.

12. GATT, *Prospects for International Trade*, September 1985 (Geneva: Press Release no. 1374). The GATT report also documented the large shift which has occurred in intercontinental trade. In 1984, for the first time, the value of North American exports to the Pacific region (including Japan) reached the same level as exports to Western Europe ($64 billion). North American imports from the Pacific region had already surpassed those from Western Europe in the mid-1970s.

13. Henry R. Nau, "The NICs in a New Trade Round," in Ernest H. Preeg, ed., *Hard Bargaining Ahead: U.S. Trade Policy and Developing Countries* (New Brunswick, N.J.: Transaction Books, for Overseas Development Council, 1985), pp. 63—83.

14. William Brock, "Trade and Debt: The Vital Linkage," *Foreign Affairs* vol. 62, no. 5 (Summer 1984), pp. 1037—58.

15. Jonathan Aronson and Paul Krugman, "Linkages Between International Trade and Financial Policies," in John Yochelson, ed., *The United States and the World Economy: Policy Alternatives for New Realities* (Boulder: Westview Press, 1985), pp. 26—44.

16. Steven Krasner, *Structural Conflict: The Third World Against Global Liberalism* (Berkeley: University of California Press, 1985).

Part III
Prospects

Seven

Second-Best Solutions

There is a middle ground between failure and success. Even while failing to revitalize the trading system, it may be possible to prevent its collapse. If multilateral trade negotiations do not succeed, what fallback positions could limit the damage to the trading system? What can be done to buy time? Or, more optimistically, is it possible to strengthen the trading system without a new GATT trade round? This chapter examines the prospects and problems of bilateral and regional negotiations as substitutes or complements to wider multilateral talks. The next chapter lays out a more far-reaching multilateral agreement.

We argue in the next chapter that the greatest gains from the negotiations could be achieved by concluding cross-sector bargains involving as many countries as possible. We refer to second-best solutions because relative to a global bargain with wide participation, they are not optimal. But as the issues are disaggregated, comparisons become more difficult to make. All issues are not conducive to wide participation. Some, like trade-distorting investment practices, may be handled better among smaller groups of countries. On other issues, some countries or groups of countries will be reluctant to contribute their share or to follow disciplines. In today's negotiations, means need to be developed to put pressure on free riders and foot draggers. Without reciprocity, the benefits of the negotiations will not be extended to non-participants.

Definitions and Background

Reciprocity is an ambiguous term in international relations. Robert Keohane distinguishes between specific and diffuse reciprocity.[1] Specific reciprocity refers to exchanges of items of equivalent value between specified partners. Obligations are clearly specified in terms of each actor's rights and duties. Diffuse reciprocity refers to situations in which equivalence is less strictly defined, and partners

119

in exchanges may be viewed as a group rather than individually.

Diffuse reciprocity is exemplified by unconditional MFN where norms and obligations are important. Specific reciprocity is exemplified by conditional MFN where country A extends to country B the same concessions it granted to country C *only if* country B reciprocates with concessions "equivalent" to those given by C to A. Conditional MFN can be used to expand trade and enhance discipline, but because only a limited number of countries are included, it is not the best that could be attained (although it may be much better than doing nothing). Specific reciprocity can also be narrower and more aggressive as when countries negotiate tit-for-tat on a bilateral basis. Many of the reciprocity bills introduced in the U.S. Congress in recent years call for aggressive reciprocity. Aggressive reciprocity is less likely to expand trade and enhance discipline and may, in fact, undermine discipline if used in a discriminatory manner.

Before discussing various second-best approaches, it is worthwhile to review arguments in favor of an unconditional MFN approach. These arguments fall broadly into two categories, economic and political, with some overlap between the two. The economic arguments center on efficiency. Nondiscrimination among sources of supply minimizes the distortions from market efficiency. Imports can come from the lowest-cost source. MFN also leads to more overall trade liberalization because liberalizing measures are generalized to all countries. And, MFN is simple to administer so that transactions costs at the border are reduced.

The political arguments for unconditional MFN center around how it tends to reduce tension among nations. From a global political viewpoint, MFN fosters sovereign equality among nations and guarantees newcomers access to international markets. The automatic extension of trade-liberalizing measures to others reduces the occasions for friction and disputes. In contrast, discriminatory arrangements can increase misunderstandings and disputes among different groupings or cause resentment on the part of outsiders. Discriminatory treatment also increases the probability that trade will be used as a weapon of foreign policy. From a domestic political viewpoint, discriminatory restrictions are more difficult to remove because they create vested interests in exporting as well as importing countries. Finally, MFN simplifies the legal and legislative burdens which proliferate if countries are treated differently. Discrimination often results in specific domestic laws being applied

differently to imports from various origins. Separate national agreements also increase the work of legislators in countries, like the
United States, where agreements have to be ratified by legislators.
Legislative action on separate agreements opens up the possibility
of domestic political bargaining which could undermine the original
intentions of the agreement.

But various exceptions to unconditional MFN exist in the trading system. Long before there was a GATT, countries entered into
Treaties of Friendship, Commerce and Navigation to codify their
bilateral trade and investment relations. Since 1981, the United
States has revived this practice by signing Bilateral Investment Treaties (BIT) with Panama, Egypt, Senegal, Zaire, Haiti, and Morocco.
(Treaties with Bangladesh, Turkey, and Morocco had been initialed
as of August 1985.) Other OECD countries have signed over 150
BITs.[2] In addition, the United States, the EC, and Japan all maintain
extensive bilateral arrangements with favored trading partners.
Such agreements can be GATT-legal and trade-promoting.

Some of the Tokyo Round NTB codes contain conditional MFN
features.[3] Only firms from countries that are signatories of the government procurement code may bid on the government projects
that are open to foreign bids. Under U.S. law, only GATT members
that are signatories of the subsidies code are entitled to the injury
test on subsidized exports to the United States. These departures
from MFN are meant to enhance discipline and be trade-promoting.

Other departures from unconditional MFN do not necessarily
promote trade or enhance discipline. Regional groupings such as
free trade areas and customs unions, divert trade as well as create it.
GATT Article XXIV, which permits regional groupings, is much
abused. It lays out specific requirements which are seldom met in
practice. The proliferation of regional groupings sets precedents for
further special deals, fragments the trading system, and damages
the interests of non-participants.

The spread of bilateral voluntary export restraints and orderly
marketing arrangements also departs from unconditional MFN.
Clearly, they restrain trade and are discriminatory.

Limited Negotiations as Partial Solutions

When the prospects for broad negotiations seemed remote, the
United States and some other industrial countries became interested in trade liberalizing agreements among smaller groups of

countries. Various plans for a "GATT-plus," a "super-GATT," or a "GATT of the like-minded" differ in detail, but have three common features. First, they are viewed as second-best alternatives to multilateral negotiations within GATT that produce the same agreements or terms. Second, they are built on the premise that if some countries, mostly in the industrial world, want to go further to liberalize trade among themselves than others, they should do so. Third, the benefits from such liberalization would only be extended to countries which participated in negotiations and accepted the discipline that emerged. Initial holdouts might join agreements after they were negotiated by contributing their fair share.[4] Specific reciprocity in the form of conditional MFN would operate to encourage those countries which would otherwise have been free riders under unconditional MFN to join.

If a new trade round does not get off the ground or stalls, those who want progress will seek it in smaller negotiations or in bilateral agreements. Indeed, limited negotiations can either substitute for or complement multilateral talks.

Should multilateral talks fail in the GATT, countries determined to strengthen the trading system and achieve liberalization might turn elsewhere and substitute limited negotiations among a smaller group of countries for the broader multilateral talks under GATT auspices. Such negotiations might be less subject to ideological disputes because only countries that believed they would benefit would participate. By keeping work on the trading system going, the bicycle might not fall over.

The danger is that unless key countries eventually joined, negotiations in smaller groups could fragment the trading system into regional groupings and undermine whatever existing authority GATT retained. Countries might leave the GATT in large numbers. At some point, so little trade might be covered by the GATT and so little respect shown for its rules that it would collapse. Fragmentation might be even more likely if countries abandoned multilateral efforts altogether in favor of a series of bilateral trade agreements. The temptation to play countries off against one another might become so overwhelming that most-favored-nation treatment would vanish from the trading system. The fundamental assumptions on which the postwar trading regime were based could be overturned, leaving countries to fight it out for the best deals they could manage.

Another possibility is that trade negotiations might move forward in the GATT and in other fora simultaneously and could complement GATT negotiations. This has occurred before. Two main variations are possible. First, on certain issues countries could proceed outside the GATT because GATT negotiations could not deal with them or they get bogged down. For instance, if LDCs refused to consider services, high technology and trade-related investment issues in the GATT, industrial countries might work on these among themselves in the OECD or some other forum. Similarly, countries might choose to negotiate on issues of particular interest to them that were moving very slowly or not at all in the GATT context. Thus, if discussions of intellectual property issues were stalled in the GATT, the United States might negotiate with Asian NICs about these topics anyway. Second, countries wishing to go further or faster than in GATT, might conduct parallel talks. Discussions of a free trade arrangement between the United States and Canada fall into this category.

Such negotiations would allow those eager to proceed to do so. Existence of separate negotiations might prompt foot draggers to expand the coverage and speed up the progress in the GATT to avoid being left behind. Tradeoffs across negotiations, not just within them, might prove possible and desirable. At the same time, parallel negotiations would be a test of the prospects for wider agreements in difficult areas. The complexity of multiple negotiations may be appropriate in an increasingly complex, interdependent world.

On some issues, like trade-distorting investment practices, limited agreements would probably be preferable. Attempts to negotiate codes of conduct for multinational corporations have bogged down in both the United Nations and the OECD. Negotiations of such issues are likely to result in the lowest common denominator in wider fora.

Limited agreements, however, will raise a host of technical, legal, institutional and political questions. Some agreements will violate GATT and some may not, although "legality" is not as precise in these matters as it is in domestic law. Accession questions will be raised subsequently when outsiders want to join after the agreement has been concluded. The relationship of the agreements to other limited agreements like the NTB codes will be complex. Those limited agreements that are part of the multilateral process may be easier to reconcile than those that substitute for it. Finally, what precedents will the agreements set for future actions or what implications will they have for future multilateral efforts? Such complexities will increase the demand for trade specialists, but will reinforce the image of GATT and trade issues as arcane, obtuse matters.

Regional or Like-Minded Arrangements

If parallel negotiations occur whether as a complement or as a substitute to wider trade talks, the first stop would probably be the OECD. Although the OECD does not include developing countries and works on a consensual basis (i.e., there is no way to penalize countries which choose not to follow its recommendations), it is frequently bolder than the GATT. During the Tokyo Round, for example, industrial countries frequently worked out their positions in the OECD before taking them into GATT negotiations. It was the Rey report of the OECD which laid the groundwork for much of the Tokyo Round.[5] LDCs use UNCTAD for the same purpose. Although such pre-negotiations are helpful for hammering out unified bloc positions, they increase the risk that different groups, each of which compromise on the lowest common denominator, will enter negotiations so far apart and with so little negotiating flexibility that compromise and agreements are impossible. The implication of this process is that in an OECD negotiation the possibility for making progress on LDC issues would evaporate. Industrial countries would pursue their own issues and interests.

Another option would be for interested countries to conduct negotiations on the margins of ongoing GATT negotiations. This would allow the negotiations to merge as they progressed, if that proved possible and desirable. In addition, it would mean that countries participating in both sets of trade talks could send only a single trade negotiating team. Similarly, multiple, compartmentalized negotiations could proceed at the GATT with different groups of countries participating in different negotiations. To some extent this happens anyway because separate working groups focus on different issues.

Another possibility is that regional negotiations might be organized. The EC is trying to create a unified market among its members and has long extended special benefits to other European countries and to many African and Asian developing countries. Such efforts could get even more attention if GATT negotiations flag. Similarly, Japan, Australia, and the NICs are seeking ways to improve Pacific trade cooperation. With or without Chinese and Indian cooperation, an Asian or Pacific Basin trade agreement could

have important implications for world trade patterns. The United States is also actively seeking to improve hemispheric trade relations. Improved trade relations with Canada and Mexico are on the agenda, whether or not GATT negotiations proceed. Even the LDCs are trying once again to improve trade relations among themselves.[6]

For four decades regional and bilateral negotiations have complemented GATT negotiations. The danger is that if progress in GATT slows or evaporates altogether while regional trade bargains proceed, the world trade system could end up being divided into blocs, each surrounded by walls of trade barriers. The benefits of global trade could be lost. Business investment made on the basis of world markets would be frustrated. Economies of large scale would be sacrificed. And what remained of GATT discipline and principles could collapse. Interregional or global trade wars could take place, with devastating impact on many economies and on global economic cooperation. No country wants a trade war, but each might believe that the others will prevent it and therefore they can continue to try to maximize their own short-term gains.

More positively, success in OECD negotiations or in negotiations that included OECD countries and self-selected LDCs could serve as a test of the benefits of freer trade. If, over time, participants seemed to benefit more than non-participants from strengthened trade rules, non-participants might be persuaded that they should also make a commitment to freer trade. The price they would pay for their delay would come in terms of slower growth in the interim. However, if the economic growth of recalcitrants accelerates outside new trade discipline, their reluctance to bind themselves to greater trade discipline would have been justified, at least in the short term.

In short, so long as the basic discipline of the trading system is intact and slowly improving, there is considerable room for parallel negotiations among smaller numbers of like-minded countries wishing to go further than the rest. Such negotiations might provide a demonstration effect, persuading others of the growth benefits that would come from greater discipline. Similarly, parallel negotiations could allow interested countries to develop greater discipline in new areas that many countries are not ready to address. More pessimistically, like-minded or regional negotiations in the absence of GATT negotiations could undermine GATT discipline, and GATT as an institution could be destroyed. Trade wars could follow.

Bilateral Free Trade Agreements

Free trade arrangements can be compatible with the GATT.[7] EC members extend to each other more liberal trade opportunities than they do to the United States. Other free trade arrangements may or may not be compatible with GATT, and when they clearly are not, the parties often seek a waiver. Former colonies and other European countries also get more liberal access to European markets than is extended to the United States or Japan.[8] In 1983, the United States extended preferential access to its smaller hemispheric partners in the Caribbean Basin. With the passage of the Trade and Tariff Act of 1984, the President has obtained the authority to negotiate bilateral free trade arrangements with other countries.

In early 1985, Congress approved a free trade agreement between Israel and the United States that will be phased in over a decade. One reason for pushing this agreement was the desire for trade liberalization. The agreement also provided the United States with an opportunity to demonstrate that a trade agreement which explicitly dealt with services could be negotiated. At the same time, it was also meant as a warning that unless progress was made toward new trade talks, the United States will go elsewhere for agreements. The United States would no longer support the multilateral trading system alone; others have to contribute their fair share.

The next step could be a U.S.-Canadian free trade agreement. The two governments could begin negotiations as early as the spring of 1986. Although there are detractors on both sides of the border, the logic of the move appeals to both governments given their economic philosophies. It could also be designed to be GATT-legal because they are each other's major trading partner. Certainly, with the large volume of trade between the two countries, a bilateral free trade arrangement makes sound economic sense. The Royal Commission estimated that over time the real income of Canadians would be increased from 3 to 8 percent as a result of free trade with the United States.[9]

The economic analysis and the political debate have been more extensive in Canada than in the United States because the stakes are higher. The prospect of gaining greater and more secure access to a market ten times as large means the potential gains are far greater for Canada, but so are the adjustments in import-competing sectors. Much of the Canadian labor movement is opposed to a trade

.nada has other concerns as well. How dependent
. want to be on the United States? Many Canadians fear
whelmed by the United States, culturally, economically,
.y, or in bilateral disputes which may arise. Will the United
hold up its side of the bargain? Can it be ensured that the
.ed States will not use the arrangement to influence Canada on
.related policy issues? Can Canada afford to make open-ended
agreements that might put them on an equal footing with Japan
(through the U.S. market) in high-technology products? (The
United States has similar concerns if Japan invests in Canada or in
those sectors where Canada has lower barriers.) Given the large
volume of U.S. foreign investment in Canada, how will those firms
react when the rules of the game change?

Procedural questions abound. Is everything put on the table at
the outset? Some Canadians would like to exclude cultural items,
import-sensitive sectors, natural resources, the auto pact agreement, parts of agriculture, and their social security and regional
development policies. The United States also has import-sensitive
sectors, and some might prefer that outstanding disputes on lumber, steel and agriculture be resolved before negotiations begin. The
more that is excluded at the outset, the less productive the negotiations will be.

But breakthroughs are possible as well. The most significant
gains could come in fashioning agreements in those areas not covered in GATT. Services, intellectual property and investment policies are the most obvious candidates. If ever there were clear and
vital linkages between trade and investment policy, it is between the
United States and Canada because of the large proportion of U.S.
foreign direct investment in Canada (over 30 percent of the U.S. total
in all industrial countries). Progress could also be made on NTBs
like subsidies and government procurement, which have not been
adequately handled by GATT.

Thorny legal, institutional, and political problems will need to
be resolved. The Canadian federal government does not exercise the
same control over the provinces as the U.S. Constitution grants control over the states to the federal government. Since many of the
provinces have adopted preferential procurement practices and
other NTBs, implementation of any agreement in these areas will
require their agreement. A succession of Ontario governments has
resisted a free trade agreement because of the potential danger of a
major disruption in its manufacturing sectors. (Ontario is the

United States' second largest trading partner, behind Canada bu, ahead of Japan.) And there is always the likelihood that the trade agreement could turn into a political football in Canada, as has happened several times in the past.

On the U.S. side, Congress will have to approve any agreement. If "fast track procedures" are used, Congress has only 60 legislative days to vote up or down a bilateral agreement submitted by the Administration. But prior to the submission of any agreement, individual members of the key committees, Senate Finance and House Ways and Means, can exert considerable influence over the outcome. Indeed, they decide whether fast track procedures can be used. If not, then the agreement is open to amendment and Congress is not required to act. How soon the United States can move on additional bilateral agreements is an open question. The Israeli free trade area legislation moved quickly through Congress. But Israel is a special case. Canada may also be a special case. Congress is wary because whenever proposals of this nature are debated, individual members end up being whipsawed by sectoral interests. Many members actually would prefer larger packages. Canada would like special provisions to get in under U.S. countervailing duties and antidumping statutes, but Israel was unsuccessful in obtaining special status.

The Administration will have to spend considerable effort convincing Congress that better trade relations with Canada are worth overriding the various domestic interests that could be hurt or that giving Canada special status under U.S. law is a good idea. (This raises a question about the U.S. Administration's strategy of concluding bilateral deals. Periodically, proposals have been floated for a Pacific Basin free trade area or for one with ASEAN. After Israel and Canada, and perhaps Mexico, what other bilateral agreements might be approved by Congress? Perhaps not many, given the sensitivity of Congress on trade with the Far East.)

With all of these potential problems, Canada and the United States are moving cautiously. Ultimately, no one knows what will be politically acceptable in either country. But the process is about to begin, and these discussions are likely to be the most complex and difficult diplomatic undertakings in the history of U.S.-Canadian relations. The process could take 2-3 years and will undoubtedly overlap with the new round. That will raise a whole host of other legal, technical, institutional, and political questions. But if ever a bilateral agreement makes sense (and could be squared with GATT)

a U.S.-Canada agreement is it.

While conceding that such an agreement may make sense in a North American context, Europe and Japan also realize that it could be one more step toward regionalization of world trade. Canadian firms would have a distinct advantage over others in selling to the giant American market. Others are concerned as well. Australia and New Zealand have expressed interest in being included within a U.S.-Canadian agreement or at least participating in the discussions. Although problems on both sides of the border make it unlikely that Mexico will join the United States and Canada to form a truly North American free trade area, slow movement in that direction is possible.

Even though bilateral free trade arrangements can be consistent with GATT, many are not. Even GATT-consistent arrangements can be destabilizing without a strong GATT. The net effect of these actions when coupled with developments in other regions is to raise the possibility of creating rigid regional trading blocs. Just as today it is very difficult to integrate the developing countries with their special and differential treatment into the world trading system, so tomorrow four or five rival trading blocs could struggle to coexist.

The experience of the 1930s shows that bilateral agreements cannot provide a stable, consistent and expanding trading system. Attempts in the interwar years to establish some predictability for trade, largely through discriminatory bilateral agreements, failed because the kind of certainty gained was illusory: the conclusion of the second or third discriminatory bilateral agreement in a series necessarily disappoints expectations created by the first. Frictions, if not downright hostility, are bound to arise between the parties. Thus, with a large number of countries trying to negotiate through bilateral agreements offering mutually incompatible privileges, predictability and stability are destroyed for everyone.

Discriminatory bilateral agreements cannot combine to form a globally consistent, stable system of national trade policies. Such a system requires effective equality of rights and obligations among countries, which can only be ensured by general acceptance of the principle of unconditional most-favored-nation treatment. This principle mobilizes large nations to support the aspiration of small ones to be treated equally. In no other way can the sovereign equality of nations which differ enormously in size and power be realized, or even approximated. For example, under a system of rules centered on the most-favored-nation principle all markets will remain open to new producers. Diffuse reciprocity is advantageous for the LDCs even if they do not always recognize it as they clamor to retain preferential treatment.

Foreign Policy Implications

Regional or like-minded groupings are an inferior alternative when compared with multilateral liberalization on a nondiscriminatory basis. Inevitably, some countries will be left out. How will they be chosen and who will decide? If national legislatures are to play a role, consider how members will be whipsawed by country interests and, disaggregating further, by sectoral interests. Furthermore, imagine what demagogues might do with other Western allies that are not following in lockstep on recent foreign policy initiatives of the United States or the NATO alliance. How will domestic trade laws be interpreted or revised vis-a-vis non-members? Some legislators, pressed by special interests, may seek to discriminate in the application of domestic law. All of this would raise trade policy from "low-level" to "high-level" foreign policy.

Regional groupings also will smack of colonialism to left-of-center politicians in many developing countries. Even for those given preferential treatment, such an arrangement would add fuel to domestic political battles in LDCs, to say nothing of the domestic political battles in countries discriminated against. A unified trading system with open markets is the strongest argument for those factions in LDCs committed to democracy and a market system.[10]

Finally, the major pillars of the trading system cannot afford to be in rival blocs. Although, the United States has expressed some frustration with the European Community (and some of its members) for slowing the multilateral process, Western cooperation remains important for strategic and security reasons and must not be undermined. The best message of security cohesion the Western nations can send to Eastern bloc nations is a flourishing, unified, nondiscriminatory system. A fragmented regional system with friction and discrimination would send the wrong signal.

***

The United States and most industrial countries would prefer to conduct negotiations under the congenial auspices of the GATT. But if too many countries or too much bureaucracy hamper progress, alternatives are available. Former U.S. Trade Representative William Brock repeatedly stressed U.S. willingness to enter into negotiations with "like-minded" countries. Secretary of State George Shultz repeated this pledge following the Bonn Summit where French President Mitterrand blocked setting a specific date to begin the negotiations. President Reagan raised the stakes in September 1985 when he proclaimed that "if...negotiations are not initiated or if insignificant progress is made, I have instructed my negotiators to explore regional and bilateral agreements with other nations."

Some limited agreements might play well in the U.S. Congress. The Administration may have trade-expanding agreements in mind, but Congress might have other ideas. Aggressive reciprocity is in fashion in the U.S. Congress. The danger is that it will be too narrowly implemented in a tit-for-tat fashion bilaterally.[11] If aggressive reciprocity legislation were to pass and become the basis for future trade actions, this would represent a radical departure from past policy and the trading system could end up fragmented.

Consider a few questions. Could the dynamism demonstrated by South Korea, Hong Kong, Taiwan, and Singapore be replicated in a fragmented trading system? We doubt it. The ascendancy of those countries to the list of the top twenty exporters and importers depended upon a multilateral trading system. Could the heavily indebted countries generate sufficient export earnings to service their debts in a fragmented trading system? Unlikely. Finally, how will the United States be able to generate current account surpluses of up to $100 billion to service its trillion dollar foreign debt in the 1990s?[12] Without an open multilateral trading system, that will be next to impossible.

The challenge in pursuing limited agreements will be to ensure that they are building blocks which allow for further liberalization either by broadening the country coverage of functional agreements or merging regional arrangements. A U.S.-Canadian agreement makes economic sense and, as long as it is nonexclusive and GATT-consistent, it could move the process of liberalization along. However, the goal of integrating the LDCs more fully into the trading system could be unattainable if "like-minded" agreements are formulated at the OECD or among industrial countries. If they are not building blocks, the limited deals could breed greater discrimination, which would further heighten trade tensions and undermine the system. Before going that route, nations should consider the mutual gains afforded by a global, multilateral bargain.

Notes

1. Robert Keohane, "Reciprocity in International Relations," *International Organization,* forthcoming, 1986. According to the Director-General of GATT, "Reciprocity is always a subjective notion which cannot be looked at in bilateral terms. It cannot be determined exactly. It can only be agreed upon and such an agreement is possible only among countries sharing a commitment to some higher principle. . . the rule of law. . . . One side alone cannot decide what reciprocity is." Arthur Dunkel, address at Hamburg, March 5, 1982, GATT Press Release No. 1312, Geneva. The principle Dunkel was referring to was nondiscrimination.

2. See *International Study on Trade in Services,* a submission by the United States Government to the GATT, December 1983, pp. 40—41.

3. For an extended discussion, see Gary Clyde Hufbauer, J. Shelton Erb and H.P. Starr, "The GATT Codes and the Unconditional Most-Favored-Nation Principle," *Law and Policy in International Business,* vol. 12, no. 1, (1980), pp. 59—94.

4. There might be "a 'GATT-plus' embracing nations prepared to trade on a freer basis than that agreed in the GATT. Second, a 'super-GATT' to unite a group of nations which would exercise trade leadership towards a more liberal system. Third, a 'GATT of like-minded' where some countries would lower barriers and invite other nations to join them." "United Kingdom Doubtful over Plans to Reform GATT," *Financial Times,* March 18—19, 1985, p. 6.

5. OECD, *Policy Perspectives for International Trade and Economic Relations* (Paris: OECD, 1972).

6. East African, Arab, and Latin American efforts to promote regional free trade groupings in the 1960s did not fare as well as Europe's attempt. The Latin American Free Trade Area continues to operate with limited success and shows some signs of renewed energy. The most promising grouping today is among the Asian NICs. The problem is that LDCs in most regions often have little export complementarity. They all try to sell and need to buy more or less the same products.

7. Free trade agreements should not be confused with Bilateral Investment Treaties.

8. In the early days of the EC, the United States made no protest of these practices, even encouraging them as an instrument to reconstruct a strong Europe. (Similarly, in the early 1950s, the United States supported Japanese preferences to keep U.S. companies out of Japan so that it could rebuild without long-lived U.S. corporate influence.)

9. Royal Commision on the Economic Union and Development Prospects for Canada, Hon. Donald MacDonald, Chairman. Report Released September 5, 1985.

10. In a speech to a special joint session of Congress on October 9, 1985, Prime Minister Lee Kuan Yew of Singapore warned against U.S. restrictive actions and asked, "Is America willing to write off the peaceful and constructive developments of the past 40 years that she made possible? Does America wish to abandon the contest between democracy and the free market on the one hand vs. communism and the controlled economy on the other, when she has nearly won the contest for the hearts and minds of the Third World?" Quoted in the *Wall Street Journal,* October 11, 1985.

11. A broad case on the advantages of following a "tit-for-tat" strategy is Robert Axelrod, *The Evolution of Cooperation* (New York: Basic Books, 1984).

12. For estimates of U.S. external indebtedness rising as high as a trillion dollars in the 1990s see Stephen Marris, *Deficits and the Dollar: The World Economy at Risk* (Washington: Institute for International Economics, forthcoming, 1985).

Eight

A Global Bargain

Certain givens dominate the trade scene. We live in an imperfect world where pragmatic realism always vanquishes elegant theory. The United States will fail to convince the rest of the world to hand their fate over to the market. Neither will the European Community or Japan convince each other, the developing countries, or the United States and Canada of the ideological rightness of their policies. The developing countries will demand a better deal, and the industrial countries will stress that successful LDCs must accept criteria by which they graduate to full reciprocity in trade relations.

What is the best that can be expected? How could a trade package be fashioned? Here we suggest how an ambitious multilateral trade round could succeed in revitalizing the trade system. Countries and leaders must recognize that they share the responsibility for getting the world economy and trading system on a sound footing. Higher growth even if it demands greater discipline is a common interest. How do we achieve these goals?

Every country, every political leader is under strong domestic pressure to encourage exports and simultaneously protect domestic producers from imports. Political reality dictates that short-term national interests usually overwhelm long-term economic interests. Thus, although the United States seeks openness abroad, Administration officials rule out concessions on textiles, apparel, shoes, steel; will not discuss labor migration; and deny that R&D funds devoted to defense projects constitute an invisible industrial policy.

Similarly, EC member states stress that the fundamental integrity of the Common Agricultural Policy is the constitutional, nonnegotiable bedrock on which the European Community stands and insist that a safeguards code is possible only if it is selective in design. Japan may bend in the wind, but MITI's role in fashioning Japanese industrial policy and Liberal Democratic Party's support of the beef, citrus, tobacco, and shipping interests will continue.

So long as excess capacity exists in labor-intensive sectors in which developing countries have a comparative advantage, industrial countries will impose on key LDCs discriminatory bilateral trade restrictions outside the GATT framework. Developing countries in turn will resist liberalization, graduation, greater discipline and the negotiation of new rules and procedures for dealing with services, high technology, trade-related investment issues, intellectual property issues, and counterfeiting.

Few analysts are optimistic about the coming trade talks. They predict a gradual extension of protectionist actions. Resisting the flood of protectionism rather than taking great strides toward liberalization is their most optimistic forecast of what can come from new multilateral negotiations. It is easy to be nay-sayers. We hope to be more constructive. Acknowledging that freer trade faces many obstacles and that progress is slow and requires significant political, economic, and social sacrifices of leaders and societies, we suggest one way to structure a mutually beneficial agreement. We try to push aside the self-righteous statements about the nonnegotiability of certain issues and focus on how deals might be cut.

In the end, negotiators frequently can set aside their parochial interests if everyone gains in the aggregate. Some countries that want to get something for nothing will try to hold up progress and force others to buy them off. However, in highly charged negotiations, free riding is becoming more difficult. Foot draggers may slow or even sabotage talks, but they are less and less likely to be paid off. Rich countries are unwilling to close discussions just to have an agreement, whatever it costs. Like-minded countries are more likely to proceed without recalcitrants.

The pressures of time limits, top-level political intervention, the spotlight of public commitment, and the fear of failure are needed to close agreements. Just as Robert Strauss fashioned a bargain at the close of the Tokyo Round in 1979 and persuaded the U.S. Congress to ratify it overwhelmingly, so future negotiators, backed by their leaders, can make breakthroughs.[1] The press will be pessimistic and negotiations long and spirited, but the final outcomes (which often get less press attention than the disagreements that precede them) can be liberal and growth-promoting. For example, most pundits expected a more protectionist bill to emerge from the U.S. Congress than the Trade and Tariff Act of 1984. Despite all the rhetoric and posturing, political leaders are pragmatists, deal-makers and problem-solvers. (They have to be or they would not have risen to their positions and responsibilities.) If they believe their country gains more than it loses from an agreement, leaders will choose one set of interests over others and push forward.

Timing and Aggregation of Issues

These negotiations could last for a decade and could take on the appearance of being continuous and never-ending. At the conclusion of the Tokyo Round, there was hope that the review committees under the various NTB codes would serve as continuing negotiating fora. Some commentators even suggested that there would be no need for another formal round. But the committees have not worked out very well. Now that the trading system is gradually deteriorating, the arguments for a round are again being advanced.

We believe that a round is essential to stem the erosion of the system, and we subscribe to the arguments about the benefits of a round. Rounds mobilize stake-holders and draw high-level political officials into the proceedings; and when deadlines are approaching, rounds force decisions. It would be better if high-level political involvement and decisions were always forthcoming, but that is not the case. For now, a round is the best alternative. Later, we suggest ways to encourage more continuous negotiations under the GATT. That is essential if GATT is to become more of a center of activity on trade policy. In the meantime we are faced with the prospect of a long, arduous negotiation. How should it be structured?

To place things in context, consider two questions: (1) Should there be intermediate deadlines or not? (2) Should issues be dealt with serially or simultaneously? Table 8.1. clarifies what is at stake. At one extreme, intermediate deadlines and serial negotiations would foster a string of separate negotiations, each relatively isolated from the others. If deemed appropriate, this would permit "watertight" separation of services and goods. At the other extreme, simultaneous negotiations on all issues without intermediate deadlines would provide a large potential for the development of packages, but also a great risk of failure. In between, serial negotiations with no pre-set time limits would keep negotiations manageable, but would minimize the chances for breakthroughs and the development of packages which cut across issue lines.

Our preference is the fourth option where negotiators deal with all the issues but set intermediate deadlines to keep on the pressure for breakthroughs. This arrangement would minimize the possibility that significant progress would be postponed until the last year of

Table 8.1
Types of Negotiations

	Intermediate Deadlines	Only a Final Deadline
Serial Negotiation of Issues	A few issues at a time dealt with for a fixed period of time. Then a new group of issues, and another. Early, unresolved issues might be revisited at the end.	Negotiators develop an order for dealing with issues but not a time frame for resolving them. As issues are settled, new ones are addressed. Overload is avoided; but harder for a wide package to emerge.
Simultaneous Negotiation of Issues	Issues dealt with in stages. Different issues might have different deadlines. Or, goals might be to resolve 3 or 4 issues by a specific date but not to specify which issues.	Negotiators would group and regroup issues as talks continued. As issues are settled, they are stockpiled or announced. Such free-form negotiations can lead to large packages, or can fail totally.

the negotiations before negotiating authority ran out. With so many complicated issues on the table, nothing of substance would probably be achieved in many areas if they were left to the last minute. Under our preferred approach, negotiators could focus on promising issues first and revisit them later if further progress is possible. Conducted in this way, the negotiations come to resemble continuous negotiations. As macroeconomic policy and political practicality permit, "harder" and "easier" issues could be rotated on and off the table. Agreements reached at the intermediate deadlines could contain contingency clauses which would abrogate concessions if progress in other areas was not achieved by subsequent deadlines. This would enhance the probability that legislatures, like the U.S. Congress, would go along with intermediate packages. But in order to bring the more difficult discussions to a close and to obtain a global package, a final deadline would need to be established. (Although we speak of a decade, a shorter deadline could be set; but then the negotiations would necessarily be less ambitious.)

Elements of a Bargain

Is a bargain possible? Can a package emerge? Yes. Although the details of what will develop are uncertain, the general framework of a workable package is predictable: each must gain, and all must sacrifice the interests of protected, inefficient domestic producers and/ or agree to limits on national sovereignty.

Under our package, the United States and Canada would get somewhat improved access to Japan and the Asian NICs and the promise of better access in other developing countries when conditions permit. The development of codes, frameworks and general principles for services, counterfeiting and intellectual property should prove possible, even if immediate liberalization in these realms is elusive. Institutional reform, stronger discipline and even limited progress on safeguards are achievable goals. Some strengthening of the NTB codes is also within reach. However, major multilateral breakthroughs on agriculture (where the United States wants improvements on trade in grain but is restrictive on dairy products, beef and sugar), high-technology products, and trade-related investment issues seem less likely. On these issues, Canada and the United States may opt for bilateral agreements.

For its part, the United States would reaffirm its commitment to special and differential treatment for the least developed countries and to the concept of unconditional most-favored-nation treatment. The United States would also need to promise that in the future it would apply and adhere to GATT rules and principles when they went against U.S. interests as well as when they supported them. In addition, the United States will have to accept the high cost of continued internal adjustment and permit greater access for LDC textiles, steel, footwear, and apparel in the U.S. market.

The most difficult problem in negotiations could be that there are no visible, political gains for the European Community. The real challenge will be to find enough to give to the Community in return for all that others will be asking. Negotiators from other countries will be hard pressed to come up with something for the Community. If enough can not be found, negotiators will have to lower their sights and the negotiations will be less productive.

European gains in any package will come at the margins. It can gain from greater access to Japan and the NICs and will benefit to some extent from progress on trade in services. (It will, however, be extremely difficult to form a European position favorable to liberalization of trade in areas such as telecommunications and insurance.) Agreements on intellectual property and counterfeiting are viewed positively in Europe. Institutional reforms could cut both ways. The EC's opposition to a stronger, legalistic GATT system is long-standing. The Community prefers ad hoc political deals, rejects or blocks dispute-panel rulings, and favors selective safeguard procedures. Some in the EC, however, would approve of an enhanced GATT. Like Japan in previous negotiations, Europe will try to buy time and will block action in areas such as safeguards and agriculture. As long as CAP remains affordable, little substantive give on agriculture is likely. Since it is always better to negotiate from a position of strength, negotiations on the high-technology sectors or services will depend upon how successful European high-technology consortia are between now and the conclusion of negotiations. If they lag, Europe will probably side with the LDCs to limit progress on high-technology issues and to keep trade-related investment issues far from center stage.

Europe is also likely to grant the LDCs somewhat greater access, but Europe's severe adjustment problems will make new concessions difficult. (However, on textiles and apparel the EC is sounding more accommodating than the United States.) Finally, the United States and Japan cannot expect much new access on the continent until Europe's economic position improves, a more integrated European market evolves, and Japan starts buying more European goods and services.

Japan will try to sit on the sidelines, supporting institutional reforms and other measures with long lead times. Now, however, unless Japan starts buying more manufactured products and sophisticated services from other industrial countries and from the NICs, others will retaliate by limiting access of Japanese products to their markets. They may also gang up on Japan to liberalize and to reform its industrial development policies. Some further relaxation of Japanese barriers which limit the import of citrus, beef, tobacco, forest products and pharmeceuticals seems possible. Overall, the Japanese will buy time, a stronger trading system and continued access for its products in return for further steps to internationalize its markets.

The gains and losses of the NICs and other developing countries, generally mirror those of the industrial countries except that they have a greater interest in a stronger system. If discipline is strengthened and market access in industrial countries is increased, the NICs benefit. To obtain concessions, the NICs will have to join the bargaining process, accepting more GATT discipline, and give up some market access both to industrial countries in capital-intensive goods and to other developing countries in traditional products. In addition, the developing countries will need to accept some sort of general principles on services and some greater discipline on counterfeiting and intellectual property. The Asian NICs will be at the center of negotiations. They will be asked to accept more responsibility for the management and functioning of the trading system. The high-debt Latin countries will be able to delay concessions longer, but will need to accept greater discipline once conditions permit. The least developed countries will be asked to give little, but they could be the major beneficiaries if market access and discipline are increased. We do not expect significant progress on tropical agriculture and commodity products in the new trade talks. Current excess capacity is too great, and the costs of price supports for LDC products would fall on unwilling citizens in industrial countries. Tempers will flare on these issues, but resolution seems improbable.

In sum, market access will be a major sticking point that will test the ingenuity of the negotiators to come up with balanced packages, including differential phase-in periods and escape clauses. Although controversial both within countries and internationally, the greatest impetus for liberalization would come if deals were cut across issues, particularly trading concessions on new issues and market access. Within industrial countries, traditional industries will not want to accept more competition from abroad in exchange for stronger disciplines and better access for the service and high-technology industries. Internationally, some worry that concessions across issue-lines would establish linkages which could be used as retaliation during future trade disputes. This could undermine existing disciplines in industrial products. But if discipline is strengthened so that respect for the system increases, this will not be a problem.

Agriculture could also be brought into cross-issue bargains but significant progress will depend upon how much the European Community and the United States are willing to change their domestic farm policies. They are the two largest exporters, and little will happen unless they move. Institutional reform is needed to make the other deals self-sustaining, but institutional reform is impossible without the European Community and the United States. There is little reciprocity involved in establishing a stronger system because it is a public good. Bargaining, however, will be intense as countries consciously understate the benefits derived from a stronger system. It is difficult to gauge the tradeoffs in advance. But institutional reform will be the critical ingredient for ensuring that the trading system evolves in response to emerging problems.

Above all else, any agreements reached will have to be flexible and contain mechanisms for updating rules and norms on a multilateral basis as circumstances change. Otherwise countries will fall back on unilateral interpretations or ignore the agreements altogether.

Disaggregating the Bargain

Talking about rights and obligations and about making and receiving concessions is not enough. Therefore, we put forward some specific ideas about what might be accomplished and how progress might take place in four critical areas that together would lead to a more flexible world trading regime. We look first at agriculture, second at issues of market access and adjustment, then at services and related new issues, and finally at questions involving discipline and institutional reform. These are likely to be the most contentious issues and will attract the most attention.

Agriculture

Agriculture will be the toughest problem. Any solution in agriculture will ultimately be a political solution—and is unlikely to last for long. Both the European Community and the United States are producing surpluses in a wide variety of agriculture products. These surpluses are being generated by support programs which provide incentives for overproduction. Since prices are propped up, price declines are not allowed to discourage production. To complicate matters, both the Community and the United States subsidize exports to reduce surpluses. Neither is likely to back down. The CAP helps hold the Community together. U.S. farm programs are almost sacrosanct as the Reagan Administration discovered when in the spring of 1985 it submitted a market-oriented farm bill to Congress and saw it dismissed immediately. For some time, the important negotiations on agriculture are going to occur within the Community and between the White House and Congress.

National governments must find other methods to achieve the numerous social and political goals which current agricultural programs try to satisfy. For example, the Reagan Administration wants to help small family farmers that have fallen on hard times when crop prices and farmland values plummeted. The current support programs cost the government almost $20 billion a year, and uncounted billions in indirect costs as sectors such as food processing pay artificially high, regulated prices. And, most of the proceeds go to large, often corporate, farmers. There has to be a better way. A more narrowly targeted financial assistance or income support program for small farmers would be less costly and more efficient. The goal should be to reduce incentives to overproduction.

Some European countries are experimenting with programs which extend support to current farmers but do not allow transfer of that support to the next generation. Something similar could be tried in the United States, perhaps an adjustment assistance program for agriculture along with deregulated prices. Even a lump sum transfer of $20,000 annually to each of the approximately 300,000 small family farms in the United States works out to just $6 billion annually—about 30 percent of current outlays—without producing distortions elsewhere in the economy. [2] If required for political reasons, such aid could be extended for 20 years, as long as every farmer knew that it would end at some specific point. This would reduce the incentive for new entrants to choose to farm.

Less costly, better designed programs which more efficiently achieve societal objectives are in every country's interest. Unfortunately, successful international negotiations to reform and rationalize agricultural policy will probably have to wait until the costs become unacceptable. At present, the best that can be hoped for is a cease-fire and a managed (political) solution. Still, efforts to improve international agriculture discipline are imperative. At minimum, work toward defining ambiguous terms like equitable share, primary product, subsidy, and representative period should begin. More ambitiously, work to bring subsidy competition in export markets under control is needed even though managed solutions will be precarious and probably short-lived. Progress may be possible on a product-by-product basis. But the emergence of new LDC suppliers and new biotechnologies which will increase productivity will probably make today's solution meaningless within a few years.

In the end, agricultural negotiations are about domestic policy. The key variable is how high the domestic price is set and by what method. Capping variable levies or easing quota restrictions may help in the short run, but they will create policy problems elsewhere. The best argument for negotiations in agriculture is that when the external consequences of domestic policies are so great, the domestic decision-making process needs external input. In the meantime, if progress is slow or nonexistent, negotiators should not let agricultural disputes prevent progress in other areas, as happened in the Kennedy and Tokyo Rounds.

Market Access and Adjustment in Basic Industries

Increased market access in labor-intensive, basic industries for LDCs, particularly in textiles and steel, should be a priority in a new round. Although the overall average tariff is low, tariffs are still high in politically sensitive, labor-intensive sectors in individual economies, and some tariff escalation on processed products remains. In the past, formula tariff cuts with limited exceptions have been the most efficient way to proceed. But if tariffs are a key issue, the negotiations will probably have to focus directly on the exceptions because for the most part that is all that remains of tariff barriers. A tougher problem will be to unwind the bilateral quota arrangements in industries like textiles and steel. Even though potential growth is tremendous, once sectoral, bilateral agreements begin to spread, it becomes extremely difficult to escape from the system of managed trade. One way would be to change the method of protection to an auctioned global quota.[3] The following proposal is based on U.S. experience, but it could be applicable in other countries as well.

An effective tariff or quota on a product will raise the domestic price above the comparable price in other countries. A major difference between tariffs and quotas is that the revenue from quotas does not go to the government. If a single global quota is established, then domestic recipients of quota licenses can seek the lowest cost supplier. When many countries produce a product, competitive pressures will hold the purchasing price down and domestic importers will earn additional revenue. Income is transferred between domestic consumers and importers. Current quota regimes in textiles and steel, however, do not work this way because they are negotiated bilaterally. When a foreign country accepts a quota, its producers can set the price, thereby transferring the additional revenue from domestic consumers to foreign producers.

How much money is involved? Firm dollar estimates are difficult to make for textiles and apparel because the negotiations involve 50 countries and cover more than 3,000 products, but some observers suggest that the U.S. transfer abroad alone could exceed $10 billion a year. As another example, the United States completed bilateral steel negotiations in early 1985 so their restrictiveness is still not known; but if the negotiations were "effective" in reducing imports to 15 percent of the U.S. market, the Congressional Budget Office calculates that it would result in about a $2 billion annual transfer to foreigners.

There are three reasons to change the way these restrictive trade regimes operate. First, the United States alone loses billions of dollars annually which could be used to finance adjustment programs. In the wake of $200 billion budget deficits, a self-financing scheme for an adjustment assistance program would improve the chance of passing legislation. If a single global quota were established and the rights were auctioned off, importers would be willing to pay for those rights because they can buy products cheaper overseas and sell them at the higher domestic price. (A market for licenses already exists—Hong Kong auctions off the right to export to the United States.) Auctioned quotas would still be restrictive, but the government would get the extra money paid by consumers.[4]

Second, a global quota with a domestic auction would be less disruptive and easier to administer than the present country-by-country negotiations. In 1983 uncontrolled textile imports into the United States increased by 40 percent because country-by-country negotiations were impossible to administer and not all-inclusive. The Administration reacted by changing import regulations in December 1983 and again in September 1984, both times causing large market disruptions. The same pattern could unfold in steel.

Third, an open auction of quota licenses (or a tariff) would allow public policy to be formulated on the basis of better information. The restrictiveness of the current quota system is not obvious to the public. Under a tariff, foreign supply can adjust and the additional cost to consumers is the tariff rate. Under quotas foreign supply is fixed, prices track demand and can increase dramatically as demand expands. Judging whether to maintain or alter current quotas is impossible because the additional cost to consumers is hidden.

An auction of quota licenses would reveal the costs of the quotas. The market value of the license would reflect the cost to the consuming public of the quota restrictions. To ensure that the program does not permanently protect the industry, a sunset provision should be established. But when the "bribe" to foreign countries to accept the quota regime is removed, their willingness to acquiesce would decrease and foreign pressure to remove restrictions would increase.

Periodic reviews also would help. The domestic policy objectives of trade restrictions, such as welfare and equity, are not now discussed openly in most countries. The public should know the reasons for, and the consequences of, its government's public policies. As emphasis or objectives change, the program could be revised.

How realistic is such a program? Lobbyists for the textile industries in the United States have testified in favor of global quotas. The question will be at what level, and the challenge will be to increase the global quota over time. More liberal, less restrictive trade should be the ultimate goal. Furthermore, if a quota's termination date was set and kept, future pressures for protection would be reduced.

Labor immobility is a major cause of the political pressure for protection. Most workers in politically sensitive industries are not very mobile occupationally or geographically, but they could be over time. Labor market adjustment assistance programs, by improving labor mobility, could reduce protectionist pressures.

The domestic debate over the new trade talks gives industrial countries a chance to reassess their labor-market policy for displaced workers.[5] Heavily protected, labor-intensive industries will have to give ground. Existing labor-market programs do not facilitate adequate adjustment in these sectors. In the United States, even a generous expansion and renewal of trade adjustment assistance would probably be insufficient to ensure passage of negotiating authority or implementing legislation. Broader, new initiatives are required.

When designing new assistance programs, dividing the workforce into age groups helps. Future labor-force entrants are the most mobile. Younger workers are less rooted to their communities and have more recent school experience than middle-aged workers. Middle-aged workers are also more likely to own their own home, to be in a two-earner family, and to be less enthusiastic about discarding acquired skills and embarking on a new career. Older workers are the least mobile, unless they qualify for early retirement.

Adjustment assistance programs generally are only effective on the margin, usually for the younger workers. Retraining and relocation are less effective for middle-aged or older workers. Still, residual jobs for the less mobile workers remain, and adjustment programs can reduce the burden on those left behind.

And, adjustment programs can perform a useful signaling function. Mobility not only occurs across jobs or regions, but over time. To the extent that new labor-force entrants see the demand for certain skills or overall labor demand in the local economy diminishing, they alter their plans. Intertemporal mobility can facilitate adjustment, but when adjustment is resisted by import protection, no signal is sent, and mobility declines.

Restrictions in steel and textiles and apparel have provided income and relative stability to individuals working in those industries for decades. Dismantling them overnight is not the answer. The best way is to set termination dates for restrictions, signaling younger workers that their industries will not provide lifetime employment and discouraging potential new entrants. Even if it takes twenty years to phase-out the restrictions, future growth will be enhanced.

Passing new adjustment programs will not be easy. Auctioning quota rights could contribute by providing the revenue to finance bolder adjustment programs and by exposing the costs of the alternative, continued protection. Those countries which take measures to facilitate adjustment and embrace change will be the beneficiaries. Those that resist change will fall behind.

Apart from increasing market access by removing existing restrictions, it is equally important to assure that market access will be sustained, except under extraordinary conditions, when safeguard actions are taken. As noted earlier, the current negotiations on safeguards are stalemated. An approach that temporarily bypasses the theological dispute over whether safeguard actions should be global or selective is needed. For example, a surveillance group established in the GATT could meet regularly to review existing measures and receive reports on new safeguards measures. Its first objectives would be to achieve transparency and to start serving as the forum for multilateral discussions. As the group amassed experience, a common viewpoint, transcending the national perspectives, might emerge in the group. In time, negotiations could be resumed to establish a safeguards code covering transparency, coverage, degressivity (phase-outs) and time limits. The absorption of the restrictive circumventions, including voluntary export restraints and orderly marketing arrangements, into the GATT system also should be a priority of the agreement.

Any new code or understanding on safeguards should also establish GATT as the forum for discussions on structural adjustment, perhaps by requiring adjustment plans to be part of all safeguards actions. Plans need not be subject to international approval, but should describe how the affected industry intends to use the temporary import relief period to restructure. This will help to concentrate the domestic pressure on the industry to become competitive. The mandate of the surveillance group could be expanded to determine whether safeguards actions were legitimate, to monitor adjustment plans to ensure that they were followed, and to make sure time limits and degressivity targets were met. If an agreement were reached and countries abided by the strictures set up by the surveillance group (instead of avoiding the process as set out by Article XIX), this would constitute a major step forward. To encourage the use of such a process, countries might waive compensation during the period under which restraints are in place. If countries did not abide by their commitments, compensation could be extracted later. Alternatively, compensation could be paid, but additional compensation could be demanded if commitments were not met.[6]

Services, High Technology and Intellectual Property

On such new issues as services, high technology, and intellectual property, negotiations will be pathbreaking and difficult. In each of these complex areas, ongoing processes and procedures should be established in order to address and resolve new issues as they arise. Initially, such arrangements will be necessary to clarify issues and to establish a common framework for proceeding. Eventually, they can be used for lodging complaints and to help mediate and settle disputes. If the review committees under the NTB codes were revamped and given higher-level attention by governments, they could serve as models.

Negotiations might proceed through three stages. In the first stage, negotiators could agree to a general commitment not to increase barriers while negotiations define the scope and objectives that will be addressed. (The pace at which new issues proceed will inevitably vary.)

In the second stage, work would focus on horizontal issues. In particular, attention would be aimed at developing codes, rules, principles and procedures parallel to those in the GATT Articles for goods. This would include dispute settlement, surveillance and complaint procedures. In addition, some of the NTB codes developed during the Tokyo Round also might be extended to services. Or, comparable codes for services might be negotiated. An umbrella code, similar to the standards code, might be most appropriate for establishing general principles. Such an approach could mean that some problems might be overlooked or not covered by rules, but exceptions have always existed in the GATT. In the third and final stage, after agreement on definitions and objectives and the negotiation of general principles, rules and procedures, negotiators would try to reduce trade barriers.

Rather than reviewing each area in which progress is desirable, we try to show the types of problems that will be faced by focusing on a key service-trade issue. A growing problem is the need to develop fair ways to manage the interaction between government-owned or controlled firms and private firms. Many approaches exist for negotiating agreements. Three possible strategies, in particular, suggest themselves. (1) An attempt might be made to extend GATT Article XVII, which deals with the behavior of state-trading enterprises, to services. We doubt that this is conceptually or politically possible. (2) Negotiators might try to extend various NTB codes (e.g., government procurement, standards, subsidy) to the treatment of government-owned service firms. This might generate some progress, particularly on a sector-by-sector basis. (3) Efforts could be focused on developing new codes outside of the GATT articles, but parallel to them.

To see how this might work out in a specific sector, consider the need to develop rules for competition between private corporations and government monopolies in the telecommunications sector. Except for the United States and Canada, almost all major countries provide telecommunications services through government-owned or controlled postal, telegraph and telephone authorities. Recently, however, the United States and to some extent Canada, Britain and Japan have been trying to promote greater competition in certain service sectors. Other countries prefer to provide services through government monopolies. Neither group of countries is likely to abandon their regulatory preferences, therefore rules need to be negotiated to allow for fair competition between public and private sector firms.[7] Telecommunications is an obvious sector where such rules are needed, but they could also apply to other service sectors. An example of what such rules might cover was suggested by the Services Policy Advisory Committee to the U.S. Trade Representative:[8]

1.) *Ability to provide services to the monopoly*: Public monopolies will frequently favor domestic service (and goods) suppliers over foreign ones. When foreign suppliers can provide quality services at competitive prices, they should not be excluded from markets through elaborate procedural, standards, or certification mechanisms.

2.) *Ability to purchase services from the monopoly*: Government-owned or controlled firms frequently favor their own subsidiaries or firms, making it impossible for others to compete. For example, in Japan, freight handling at airports discriminates against non-Japanese carriers and, in Europe, airline reservation systems exclude schedules of U.S. carriers. A related problem is that horizontally-integrated monopolies may use cross-subsidies to distort their pricing, making it difficult for U.S. firms to compete. For example, governments are willing to permit state-run airlines to lose money, in order to funnel tourist dollars into the economy.

3.) *Ability to compete with the monopoly*: Here there are two related issues. First, unless the monopoly allows the foreign service provider to "plug in" to the underlying systems, there is no way it can compete. But, even when permission to plug in is granted, the monopoly may use its dominant position to limit competition. For example, it does U.S. data communication firms no good to receive permission to provide enhanced services if they cannot use the basic service network on a fair basis. Yet the providers of basic services are likely to be government monopolies moving into the provision of enhanced services. They can extend their monopoly by restricting access to their old services.

4.) *Ability to compete in third markets*: Some government-owned or controlled service firms receive significant subsidies that allow them to undersell U.S. firms. For example, Korean construction firms are subsidized when they bid for foreign contracts. At the same time, the Reagan Administration plans to curb Eximbank funds that assist U.S. firms operating abroad in matching foreign credit subsidies. Similarly, there is the possibility that the opening of the Intelsat system to more competition, as the U.S. proposes to do, will help subsidized French and British satellite monopolies get a larger share of the Atlantic communication traffic while giving up very little of what they now dominate.

The bulk of trade in services is between industrial countries. Therefore, industrial countries are keen to deal with services issues even if the LDCs refuse to participate. One key aspect of service negotiations might focus on the right of market access for foreign firms. Efforts to assure nondiscrimination, national treatment and the right to do business for foreign service suppliers is a central agenda item for service discussions. (Those concepts that are established for goods in the GATT need to be revised and applied to services. This is not straightforward because many countries choose to provide key services through government-owned or controlled monopolies and because the line between trade and investment in services is not as sharp as for goods.)[9]

What can be expected on other new issues? Although the U.S. business community places investment high on their priority list, we do not expect the new trade talks to do much more than go on record as favoring more study of trade-related investment issues. Progress on counterfeiting and intellectual property is more promising. Successful negotiations on counterfeiting should prove possible. Intellectual property issues will be more difficult, but progress seems likely in extending the international framework of trading rules to cover copyright, patent and trademark protection. Harmonization and codification of intellectual property rules and the establishment of dispute-settlement procedures are desirable. Intellectual property issues will be central to trade in services and high-technology trade issues. Integrating them into the trade regime is important.

Services and intellectual property issues have never been covered by multilateral trade rules. As services grow in importance within the world economy, extending the trade regime to cover them is a priority objective. As this process unfolds, countries must first halt the proliferation of new barriers so that they can establish appropriate rules and procedures necessary to reduce obstacles to trade in services in the future. Moreover, it is imperative that new rules and procedures be drafted so that they will be able to continue to function, evolve and be relevant as the world information economy continues to develop.

Institutional Reform

The GATT system is at present not discharging one of its key functions: to protect governments against themselves by providing help to policy-makers in withstanding pressures from special interests. If GATT rules and procedures were well respected, they could be cited as international obligations that, if broken, would result in reprisals and redress. But now, when policy makers and legislators are confronted by constituents with special interest requests, GATT commitments offer little firm ground on which to argue for the general interest, as opposed to special interests.

Institutional changes are needed to strengthen trade discipline and to improve trade policy formulation both internally and internationally. Internal and international reforms could be mutually reinforcing. Stronger international discipline could reduce the number of unilateral actions. Internal decisions resulting in fewer unilateral actions could enhance the credibility of the system and its discipline.

Disraeli once remarked that in international trade, there are no principles, only interests. True enough, but the problem is that not all interests are heard from. Only the import-sensitive industries actively plead their case. The stake-holders in open trade (exporters, retailers and consumers) are relatively silent. Furthermore, in most public discussions of trade protection, the right questions are seldom asked. If legitimate issues of adjustment or national security are involved, are import restrictions the most efficient policy available? Given the fundamental asymmetries in trade policy formulation, each country needs to adopt a better accounting framework for the costs and consequences of restrictionist actions. The primary consequences of trade restrictions are felt by different groups within countries, not between countries. Better information on the consequences would help policy makers to make better-informed judgements. The GATT Wisemen's report recommended that all countries develop and adopt a protection balance sheet or a protection impact statement to improve internal trade policy formulation.[10] One example of how such an analysis might work was given by President Reagan in his denial of import relief to the shoe industry. Citing additional costs of up to $3 billion to American consumers, he rejected import relief, providing retraining instead. Such calculations are now made in the United States on an ad hoc basis but there is no mechanism for systematically providing them.

Formulating trade policy within countries should also be opened up and subject to more public debate and scrutiny. The dangers of secrecy and administrative discretion are greater than those of more open procedures. The open approach, exposing conflicting interests, also shields politicians better against protectionist pressures. The two examples which come closest to such an open approach are the International Trade Commission in the United

States and the Industry Assistance Board in Australia. Both are useful as "magnifying glasses" to highlight the domestic distribution of the costs and benefits of trade restrictions.

At the international level, several institutional reforms are needed to update and enhance the GATT; the adjudication of disputes and enforcement of rules needs strengthening; rules on subsidies and unfair trade need to be revamped; GATT should become more of a forum for mediation and conciliation of trade policy issues that are not explicitly covered by existing rules; GATT should be reformulated so that the system can respond to problems as they emerge. Ultimately, GATT needs to become more respected so that it can be leaned upon by national policy makers.

Governments need to be held more accountable for their trade policies. They should be required regularly to explain and defend their overall trade policies. The GATT Wisemens' group recommended that each year a panel representing three to five governments should be established to review a GATT Secretariat report on the trade policies of each of the major industrial countries (less frequently for smaller countries), subject its representatives to questioning, and make recommendations. Countries participating on the panel would differ for each country under review. This surveillance procedure is similar to the OECD economic reviews and could also serve to review existing restrictions and safeguard actions. To ensure action, the Secretariat should also be given more authority to take initiatives and to respond to outstanding problems.

No one is tending the trading system at the present time. A strong independent international component is needed to operate in the general interest and enforce the rules and norms. Trade rules and discipline are a public good. What is needed is a traffic cop to hand out tickets. The GATT Secretariat should be empowered to initiate studies of national trade policies; to collect, maintain, and publish comprehensive information on trade policy measures and actions. It should also be given the authority to call meetings and set agendas.

To promote confidence in the system, dispute-settlement panels should be set up and should complete their work more speedily and should always clearly indicate the rationale for their findings. One of the delays in dispute-settlement cases occurs when a panel is being put together. The GATT Wisemen's report called for establishment of a permanent roster of non-governmental experts familiar with GATT matters who could be called on to serve on panels. A cadre of expert panelists would help to minimize the political influence on dispute panels which is inherent in the current process because countries are allowed to suggest or reject panelists. Such a panel of experts is similar to the administrative law judges in the U.S. labor relations cases and the board of experts which serves the U.S. Nuclear Regulatory Commission. Dispute-settlement procedures would also be improved if the Director-General of GATT were authorized to initiate mediation and conciliation at an early stage in disputes. Currently, cases remain unresolved for months until action is begun under dispute-settlement proceedings.

GATT rules on subsidies are not as explicit or as fully accepted as the rules on tariffs. Subsidies go to the heart of the fairness question. More work needs to be done to define what subsidies are and when it is legitimate to use them. In the absence of multilateral agreement on the use of subsidies, there will be separate national definitions. These national definitions are likely to conflict. Even with a more explicit multilateral agreement, subsidies used for domestic purposes will always create empirical questions about the extent to which they affect trade and cause injury to foreign economies. To resolve these questions and the disputes they are likely to create, GATT needs to become more of a forum for mediating and reconciling trade disputes arising from domestic subsidies and subsidies used to promote the development of industrial sectors.

GATT's role as a forum for continuous negotiation should be developed. For GATT to be effective, political commitment and more frequent eye-to-eye contact to increase peer pressure are required. To keep abreast of recent developments and to minimize potential conflicts in this rapidly changing world, trade ministers should meet more frequently as their financial counterparts do at the IMF and World Bank annual meetings or as the leading monetary authorities do monthly at Basel under the auspices of the Bank for International Settlements. A standing ministerial-level body should be established to serve as an executive committee to move issues along or to address them before they become full-blown. To solve the constituency question an existing body, like the Interim Committee of the IMF, could be used as a model. In order to examine trade and finance issues in a more consistent fashion, it would be useful if trade and finance ministers both attended the new body together at periodic intervals. It would also be useful if trade ministers attended meetings of the IMF Interim Committee on a regular basis.[11]

One way to strengthen the system would be to unify it. Industrial countries argue that developing countries have been free riders for too long and that it is time to stop debating who is developing and who should graduate. They feel there needs to be a greater acceptance that we are all in the same boat and that all countries have contributions to make in raising growth. The trick will be in defining criteria for graduation. Developing countries are understandably reticent to accept greater responsibility, but if they felt that they were being integrated into an enhanced system, they may be willing. If these proposals for institutional reform were adopted, GATT would be different. It would no longer be a rich man's club, but would provide more discipline over all countries, large and small alike.

In sum, institutional reforms are essential so that other steps taken to liberalize trade and strengthen rules are self-sustaining. Although stiff, sure, swift sanctions would be more effective in deterring trade policy violations, these reforms are the most that can be hoped for in the immediate future. At times, the European Community and the United States have both opposed strengthening GATT and the trading system in the past. The changes will not occur without pressure from the smaller and medium-sized countries, which could demand that institutional reform be part of the bargain. The establishment of graduation procedures would be one thing the developing countries could give in return for institutional reform. After all, a stronger system is the best protection for the weak against the strong.

First Steps and Interim Measures

In order to get a round off on the right foot, all participants will have to ante up something to show good faith. The usual platitudes now enshrined in numerous OECD Ministerial and Summit communiqués call for a standstill on new restrictions and consideration of rollbacks of existing restrictions.

As a first step, the heads of state of the major industrial countries should issue a credible statement promising that they will not take any action (over which they have discretion) for a given period of time. Separate statements by heads of state, ideally led off by President Reagan, would help foster confidence and encourage others to join negotiations.

In our view, just putting everything on the table would be a good first step along with a standstill and with a commitment to look at all existing problems in working groups. Separate working groups or negotiating committees could be established in each of the separate issue areas. Eventually, some things will probably be excluded, but in the short run there should be no sacred cows.

On safeguards, a survey of existing restrictions would be a start. Similarly, upgrading the review committee for the Tokyo Round subsidy code would be useful. Groups dealing with new issues or rules changes will spend the initial period defining issues and exchanging suggestions. They will move slowly and attract less attention.

One way to attract more attention to the entire negotiation, particularly among high-level political officials, would be to have each country table a list of actions on an item-by-item basis that it requests other countries to take. Such request lists would be exchanged and negotiations would begin in earnest. This structure would work best for questions of market access, but it could also be used later on in services and under the codes after rules have been clarified. Countries could also stipulate what actions they would take if a particular request was denied. Such a request procedure would have the salutary effect of mobilizing the private sector behind items of interest to them that they have been seeking from foreign countries. That, in turn, would engage higher-level political officials. To be sure, there are risks in such an approach, but exposing and highlighting the domestic conflicts of interests on trade issues may be the only way to move ahead. Entrenched import-competing interests are already mobilized; what is lacking is the countervailing force.[12]

Two problems with such a approach will be: (1) how to handle those trade policy actions that will come up but over which the executive has no discretion and (2) how to handle illegal restrictive measures taken outside of the GATT, because traditionally no concessions or reciprocity are required for illegal measures. One way to avoid the second problem would be to have separate request procedures for legal and illegal measures. There are certainly enough illegal measures to warrant a separate group. Resolution of the first problem will be more difficult and will require building consultation and mediation procedures into the request process.

The problem with a protracted negotiation will be how to hold it together for its duration. We suggested one strategy above: to provide intermediate deadlines. As intermediate deadlines approached, political and public pressure could be applied to all separate groups to come to at least a limited agreement. Such pressure would also help foster cross-sector deals which are necessary if significant progress is going to be made to develop packages acceptable to all major participants. Similarly, existing mechanisms and interim disciplines developed during the talks could be used to keep up the pressure. Governments could bring cases under the NTB codes, invoke safeguard actions and appeal to dispute-settlement proceedings. Such actions will occur in any event, and they are more likely to be resolved quickly during a multilateral negotiation. Such actions could also be strategically focused to prompt decisions and move negotiations forward. Indeed, to keep the interest and attention of high-level political officials over the course of a decade will require all these tools.

**

To conclude, despite all the domestic constraints that we have pointed to throughout this book, we believe progress is possible. We are aware that we are laboring under the weight of controlled schizophrenia. We believe this is a constructive malady. To descend into the doldrums of pessimism helps nothing. Pollyanna optimism is equally useless. The key to progress is in accepting that the world is complex and getting more so, that there are no perfect solutions to the trade problems that bedevil us, and indeed that there is no such thing as a coherent trade policy (just as it is impossible for any country to conduct a coherent foreign policy). Therefore, heads of state and their negotiators have to do the best they can to tackle the deep-seated, social and cultural factors that lie at the heart of today's major trade problems. The tension that is created when negotiators are subjected to cross-cutting pressures is positive. It clears the mind and helps promote more creative solutions. Quite simply, growth, jobs and the future of the world economy are at stake. Trade problems need to be solved. Many of them are ready to be solved. We have the capacity to solve them. Let's get on with it.

Notes

1. Gilbert Winham, "Robert Strauss, the MTN, and the Control of Faction," *Journal of World Trade Law*, September-October 1980, pp. 377—97.

2. The figure of 300,000 is derived from data from the Department of Agriculture and the Internal Revenue Service to determine the number of small farmers who receive the bulk of their income from farming. Even if support were extended to three times as many farmers, it would be less than current direct outlays.

3. For a more detailed analysis, see C. Michael Aho, "U.S. Labor-Market Adjustment and Import Restrictions," op. cit. Gary Clyde Hufbauer and Howard Rosen in "Trade Policy for Troubled Industries," Institute for International Economics, forthcoming 1985, make a strong case for auctioned quotas or the conversion of quotas to tariffs. Gary Clyde Hufbauer, Diana Berliner and Kimberly Elliot of the Institute for International Economics are conducting a major analysis of the degree of restrictiveness of most outstanding U.S. restraints, *Trade Protection in the United States: 31 Case Studies*, forthcoming 1985.

4. A tariff with the same restrictive effect could generate the same amount of revenue. The advantage of an auctioned quota in the United States is that the market, rather than Congress, would determine the degree of restriction, at least initially. If nontariff barriers were to be converted to tariffs, Congress would get into the act.

5. Most economists and policy makers believe that market forces provide the most efficient method for allocating resources. The government's role is to correct market failures where they exist and to provide a policy framework which relies as much as possible on market forces. But labor market policy is at the intersection of economic and social policy and other objectives are involved. Government intervention is likely in one way or the other. It cannot be assumed away. The key is to intervene in the least costly way. For a discussion of market-consistent adjustment initiatives and related policy issues, see C. Michael Aho, "U.S. Labor Market Adjustment Policies in a Changing World Economy," in Catherine Stirling and John Yochelson, eds., *Under Pressure: U.S. Industry and the Challenges of Structural Adjustment* (Boulder: Westview Press, 1985), pp. 219—260.

6. This is similar to the proposal made in the GATT Wisemen's report. "The phasing-out process for safeguard measures should be subject to review in the GATT, perhaps in a standing "adjustment committee" created specially for this purpose. This would ensure that countries were living up to the phase-out commitments; if they were not, exporting countries could have grounds for additional compensation." (p. 42—43)

7. The question has been raised, however, whether deregulation is contagious. For a discussion of the impacts of deregulation on competition in international telecommunications, see Peter F. Cowhey and Jonathan D. Aronson, "The Great Satellite Shoot Out," *Regulation* (May-June 1985), pp. 27—35 and Peter F. Cowhey and Jonathan D. Aronson, "Trade in Communications and Data Processing" in Robert Stern, ed., *Proceedings of the Third Annual Workshop on Canada/United States Relations* (Toronto: Ontario Economic Council, forthcoming 1986).

8. "Chairman's Report on a New Round of Multilateral Negotiations," submitted to the United States Trade Representative, May 15, 1985.

9. See Jonathan D. Aronson and Peter F. Cowhey, *Trade in Services: A Case for Open Markets*, (Washington, D.C.: American Enterprise Institute, 1984) and Harald B. Malmgren, "Negotiating International Rules for Trade in Services," *The World Economy*, vol.

8, no. 1 (March 1985), pp. 11—26 for more detailed ideas about possible approaches to liberalizing trade in services.

10. GATT Wisemen's report *Trade Policies for a Better Future: Proposals for Action*, GATT, March 1985. The GATT Wisemen's group made several recommendations designed to strengthen discipline and to reduce frictions in trade policy. The recommendations by this group of eminent, practical people from outside trade policy circles imply a great deal for institutional reform of the trading system. But as one scholar noted, you have to read the black print below the recommendations (which are in green bold-face). That is where the meat is. The report contains a detailed framework for evaluating the costs and benefits of trade restrictions in an Appendix.

11. Ibid. "There is a clear need to create greater contact in GATT between governments, at a senior level including more frequent Ministerials...A standing GATT Ministerial-level body of limited membership should be established. Such a body should enable the Ministers who set the course of their countries' trade and economic policies to come together frequently to share views and information, to help each other to resist protectionist pressures at home, and to carry forward international cooperation." (p. 48) The report also "urged the IMF Interim Committee to meet at regular intervals with both trade and finance ministers in attendance" (p. 49).

12. The promise of greater foreign market access can help to mobilize the self-interest of exporting sectors to favor trade liberalization, but there is a more subtle reason as well that exporters should favor it. Reducing a tax on imports is equivalent to reducing a tax on exports. As it was put in GATT, *Prospects for International Trade* (Geneva: Press Release no. 1374, September 1985), "Since imports and expanding exports go hand in hand, a global process of trade liberalization would give a *double* boost to production and employment in the export sector of each country—once as a result of reductions in foreign barriers and once as a result of reduction in its own country's barriers" (p. 27).

Nine

Conclusion: Outlook

Trade talks can succeed. If countries cooperate, higher growth and greater discipline are possible. These two goals go hand-in-hand. Neither is possible without the other. No country will sacrifice its own growth prospects for the insubstantial benefits of stronger trade rules. Yet national and international growth prospects will suffer unless the trading rules are overhauled and made relevant to today's fast-changing world economy. To get ready for the 1990s, trade talks will have to address and make progress on both fronts at once.

The ten policy challenges described in Chapter 2 will make new negotiations different and more difficult than those in the past. Growing interdependence, the decline in the ability and will of the United States to dictate terms, the proliferation of industrial policies and the emergence of excess capacity in many sectors at a time when world economic growth is slowing puts profound pressure on negotiators. In addition, negotiations will be different because traditional sectoral distinctions are breaking down, global corporate competition is changing, new types of trade barriers have replaced tariffs as the focus of attention, services need to be addressed, and product-life cycles are shortening as the pace of change accelerates. These challenges make it more difficult to build domestic coalitions favoring trade liberalization, particularly because employment and adjustment problems are critical everywhere and are related to broad domestic reforms which ultimately will determine whether trade can be liberalized.

As new trade talks begin, opportunities and pitfalls abound. We expect progress because the alternative is deterioration of the trading system and with it the world economic system. How long the system will hold together without reform is impossible to predict, but few careful analysts believe that the trading system can survive indefinitely without a major overhaul. However, no country, including the United States, is willing to accept the brunt of the costs of renovation. Each would like a free (or at least a subsidized) ride. That's impossible. Therefore political leaders around the world will have to summon up courage and persuade their countries that they must contribute something if everyone is to benefit.

The most critical moves must come from, and the most ominous signs are coming from, the United States. Over 300 protectionist bills have been introduced into Congress in 1985. Members of Congress are currently unprotected from constituent requests for special treatment. They are only hearing one side of the story. The overvaluation of the dollar has eroded the domestic consensus in favor of trade liberalization as exporters facing unprecedented competitive problems are not lobbying for open trade. GATT is not now effective as a means to deflect special interest requests. The feeling is widespread on Capitol Hill that the United States is not vigorously enforcing its existing trade laws. Congress wonders who is in charge of trade policy. Sentiment is brewing to pass some legislation restricting imports and/or rewrite U.S. trade laws expanding the definition of unfair trade practices and to make retaliation mandatory when unfair trade practices are found.

In the face of the possibility that Congress will pass some form of restrictionist legislation, President Reagan has reassessed his trade policy and overall international macroeconomic policy. He instructed the Secretary of Treasury to work together with the other major countries to bring the dollar down. This represents a change in the Administration's position. He has also instructed his USTR, Clayton Yeutter, to work with Congress to put together a trade bill with revisions in U.S. trade laws acceptable to the Administration and with a request for negotiating authority for a new round of trade talks. Whether a trade bill will pass in a form acceptable to the President is uncertain. Much bargaining needs to be done. But at least the process is beginning in earnest. Whatever else emerges from the President's new trade strategy, new trade talks will be a central element. And even if Congress should pass a restrictionist bill, the President has said he will veto it and the veto can be sustained with only 34 votes in the Senate. Passage of a restrictionist bill with a Presidential veto might not be all bad. Indeed, a veto with the threat of an override might be just the leverage the Administration needs to get recalcitrant countries to move forward in negotiations.

The President's strategy, even if arrived at late in the game, is a sound one. A new round of trade talks will both begin to address the manifold problems of the trading system and provide protection for legislators confronted with special interest requests. To take unilateral actions would jeopardize the multilateral talks. But the Congressional pressures are not going to go away, and the Administration is going to have to re-establish its credibility on trade issues by vigorously pressing other countries. If the priorities for action are selected carefully, that could also have the salutary effect of mobilizing domestic interests behind the Administration's strategy. But only in a multilateral context can such strategies be effectively employed. Then once in the round, the Administration will have to begin to address the labor adjustment problems inherent in granting more market access to import competition. Although the President is not out of the woods yet, he is moving down the right path. What remains to be seen is whether he has the commitment and resolve to see it through.

To revitalize the trading system, rhetoric will have to give way to pragmatism. Ultimately, a package that is perceived as fair to all major interests needs to be developed. That is still years away. For now, countries must get things started one step at a time. We believe that the chances of increasing growth and strengthening trade disciplines will improve if political leaders and their negotiators keep in mind these eight observations.

First, *promote growth and discipline; worry less about free trade and protectionism.* Progress is more likely if the focus is on positive goals instead of sterile debates. Trade liberalization enhances economic growth. Greater discipline can reduce uncertainty and lead to an expansion of trade, investment and growth. By contrast, free trade, like absolute zero in physics, cannot be attained. Freer trade is all that can be achieved. In an interdependent world where sectoral boundaries blur and national industrial policies conflict, free trade is only useful as an ideal to help in making comparisons. Protectionism is also relative. Legitimate social, cultural and security concerns will always persuade governments to protect key sectors to varying degrees. Countries will continue to promote their own development even if this means protecting their firms against foreign imports and subsidizing their firms' exports. In order to protect against widespread abuse of these practices, negotiators need to develop trade practices and procedures that are responsive and respected so that trade issues are resolved with a minimum of friction. Otherwise the system's credibility will continue to suffer.

Second, *learn to live with complexity; stop trying to revolt against interdependence.* The world is changing. A return to a simple, isolated existence is impossible even if it were desirable. The world in which the GATT was created is gone forever. As interdependence increases, domestic economic policies cannot clash successfully with world economic trends. Nations can no longer follow independent trade, monetary, and investment policies. Shifting corporate structures and the emerging world information economy provide great opportunities for growth and job creation but are making regulation much more difficult to fine tune domestically or internationally. The line between goods and services is getting harder to distinguish. Similarly, tariffs have declined in importance as obstacles to trade and have been replaced by various sorts of nontariff barriers. Too often government officials and negotiators are trying to solve yesterday's problems. Such myopia creates as many problems as it solves. Therefore, negotiators need to learn to deal with the world as it is and as it is becoming and not base their actions and positions on a view of the world that is no longer relevant.

Third, *make sure the underlying principles are right; stop being overly rigid and legalistic.* The increased complexity of the world economy and of world competition makes it necessary to focus more on general principles and less on details. Unless the trading system is moving in the right direction, nothing much will help. Because the rate of economic change is accelerating, detailed rules are likely to become outdated and inappropriate more rapidly than in the past. Overriding principles (e.g., nondiscrimination, transparency and reciprocity) with mechanisms for updating rules are necessary to keep the trading system vital and relevant.

Some computer programs now rewrite themselves. They learn from experience and adapt to improve their performance. For example, chess-playing computer programs now defeat all but the best players in the world. The same concept needs to be introduced to trade rules. Trade rules cannot be written in stone. They must be allowed to adapt and change as the world economy and the world trading system change. Following the letter of the law is not helpful when the world for which the law was designed is gone. The United States remains the foremost advocate of a legalistic approach to trade rules. This approach needs to be tempered. The application of rules should depend more on the circumstances of the problem. Nevertheless, ways need to be found to prevent cheating. In the future, prudent application of safeguards and escape clauses may have to replace strict application of rules. However in emphasizing adaptability, care must be taken not to sacrifice predictability. That is why it is not contradictory to strengthen mediation and conciliation procedures and mechanisms for seeking redress and for enforcing norms.

Fourth, *start the process of reform now; don't wait for the crisis*. In the past, major reforms were only possible in the face of crisis or collapse. Interdependence makes risking collapse before instituting reforms particularly dangerous. Today, all countries would suffer in a collapse. If depression strikes the United States and the major industrial countries or if the major LDCs are unable to service their debts, all countries will suffer the consequences. Work needs to begin to extend and adapt the trading system to cover the areas that are not now covered within the GATT. It is equally important to pull some of the sectors that have escaped from GATT discipline back into the system and to strengthen GATT discipline. Each country can contribute something now to preserving and promoting the general good, or they may have to pay much more later to restore a broken system.

Fifth, *U.S. leadership is critical*. Some one must take the lead—only the United States can do this and it must be done at the highest levels. Ronald Reagan needs to be personally involved. As former U.S. Trade Representative Robert Strauss has put it, the President's popularity is not to be saved; it should be spent in order to achieve breakthroughs on trade. In addition, the President must make clear that he has confidence in and will actively support his trade negotiator. Moreover, since the United States will have a new President before negotiations are far under way, the next President and perhaps the one after that will need to make trade a continuing priority. This is needed domestically, otherwise Congress might seize the initiative and try to set trade policy. For if U.S. leadership wavers or falters, other countries will pick up the cue and efforts to move forward will be undermined.

Sixth, *the United States cannot lead alone*. Even as the United States must redouble its efforts to lead, others need to increase their contributions as well. As power diplomacy has faded, the need for cooperation, coalitions and bargaining increases. Unless in today's highly pluralistic world the other pillars of the system, the European Community and Japan, accept their responsibilities, no progress is possible. They must take a less parochial attitude and increasingly assume the burdens and responsibilities commensurate with their size and stake in international trade. This means that the EC should stop holding efforts at trade liberalization and strengthening discipline hostage to the resolution of existing internal and external disputes. For Japan, this means taking further unilateral steps to open its markets and, more fundamentally, to change the social and political attitudes that have made its market so impervious to outside penetration and to dispel the widespread perception that it uses unfair practices to gain competitive advantages. The NICs must also accept that they have responsibilities for maintaining the system and cannot expect to get the benefits of access to industrial-country markets without doing their share to open their markets and support trade rules. Since fundamental social policies and objectives are involved in all the major countries, other heads of state must become active participants. A far-reaching global bargain can only be struck at the higher levels.

Seventh, *reforms must be phased in slowly; domestic political constraints are growing, not decreasing.* Even as we write of progress, it is clear that reform can only be implemented in an ordered, step-by-step manner. Countries will accept more competition and discipline, but only a little bit at a time. Domestic accommodations are needed and domestic adjustment needs time to work. However, limits and schedules have to be developed for adjustment so that uncompetitive sectors are not protected indefinitely to the detriment of their own consumers and the rest of the world. Long phase-in periods are another reason to begin the process now and not delay. Both the long phase-ins and the long duration of the negotiations will also require flexible, continuing processes in GATT to monitor developments and to deal with potential problems before they become full-blown.

Eighth, *mobilize the stakeholders in an open trading system.* The fate of the trading system depends upon domestic political decisions. Unless the key stakeholders are mobilized to encourage more liberal trade at home and abroad, long-term trade prospects will dim. Multilateral negotiations can help to mobilize the stakeholders in all countries, but internal reforms are needed as well. Trade negotiations are held among the nations of the world, but fundamentally they involve internal disputes with distributional consequences. To maximize the chances of progress, the round should be structured to highlight those domestic conflicts of interest. Internal reforms which increase domestic awareness about the positive as well as the negative consequences of trade liberalization would help the negotiations to move forward.

Countries should adopt open procedures and require cost/

benefit analyses of changes in trade policy similar to the environmental-impact statement now required in some countries. Where there are negative consequences for workers, firms, and communities, governments have a responsibility to ameliorate the adjustment burden for those who suffer the consequences of trade liberalization. But that amelioration should be done in such a way that the governments' responsibility to the other stakeholders in trade liberalization is also met. Internal and international reforms would be mutually reinforcing. Stronger international discipline would reduce the resort to unilateral action. Internal decisions resulting in fewer unilateral actions would enhance the credibility of the international discipline. Both would work hand-in-hand to restore confidence in the efficiency and the efficacy of the trading system.

* * *

Needless to say, a great deal needs to done to reform the international trading system. It will not be easy and it will not happen overnight, but the stakes are too high not to try.

Institutions, like human beings, seldom mark time. The GATT will observe its fortieth birthday in 1987. Much has changed since its inception. But now, as then, the world is sorely in need of more international cooperation on trade matters. In the absence of efforts to make progress on the important international trade issues, the system will regress further. If nations of the world do not begin to focus on these pressing trade problems, the world faces the possibility of a repeat of the 1930s, when the collapse of the trading system contributed to the length and severity of the depression.

Although the problems confronting the trading system are grave, failure to deal with them is a prescription for disaster. If all countries would put aside their long-standing differences and be bold and forthcoming, all countries will gain and a better future is possible. Let us begin that long and arduous process.

Appendix I

U.S. Goals for New Multilateral Trade Negotiations, United States Trade Representative, July 9, 1985

The United States believes that there is an urgent need for action to improve and strengthen the international trading system, which is under severe strain. Pressures on governments to restrict imports are increasing, partly as a result of serious adjustment problems in key industries but also in large part due to the absence of an effective dispute settlement mechanism and the lack of meaningful international discipline over import restraints and export subsidies. These pressures give rise to trade distortive actions that prejudice the interests of trading partners and cause them, in turn, to take similar restrictive measures. This current trend needs to be reversed to secure the expansion of world trade, support global economic growth and continue the improvement of worldwide living standards. Maintenance of open markets also would assist developing countries in meeting their debt obligations and supporting their development efforts.

The GATT work program initiated in 1982 covers most of the pressing issues. This work program is reaching a stage where further progress will depend on the initiation of negotiations. These negotiations, to be conducted under the auspices of the GATT, would be open to any contracting party wishing to participate. In the U.S. view, the negotiations should aim to:

—strengthen and develop trading rules to better attune them to current and future trading environment;

—expand the exchange of goods through the reduction of trade barriers to raise standards of living; and

—develop a set of rules applicable to trade in services.

This paper lays out the initial view of the United States on the first set of issues to be dealt with in the negotiations. It is based on preliminary consultations with our private sector. We expect to consult further with them, and with Congress, in the months ahead.

165

Additional or modified proposals for negotiations may emerge out of this process.

We believe a meeting of senior officials is needed to initiate an evolving process of international consensus building on the issues to be addressed. In this context, the United States is prepared to consider trade issues proposed by other countries.

U.S. Objectives for Negotiations Dealing with Trade in Goods

I. Improving the GATT System.

The United States is seriously concerned about the erosion of GATT discipline and believes that high priority should be assigned to strengthening the GATT system by means of improving multilateral disciplines. Specifically, we believe that agreement should be sought in the following areas:

—Dispute settlement. The U.S. believes that if the international business community and contracting parties are to retain confidence in the GATT system, an expeditious and effective dispute settlement mechanism is essential. The current mechanism does not provide this, and the negotiation should aim to achieve a vastly improved mechanism.

—Agriculture. The work in the Committee on Trade in Agriculture has established a solid framework for negotiations, which should provide an effective discipline on import restrictions and export subsidies in agriculture. The United States favors greater discipline over agriculture trade practices and elimination of any permanent exceptions for agricultural trade from GATT rules.

—Import Restraints. The United States believes that it is important to establish an effective GATT discipline over all actions taken to restrain imports. As a first step, we seek an agreement on the application of the four building block principles—transparency, surveillance, limited duration and degressivity—to all import restrictive actions taken by all contracting parties. These disciplines would apply to new measures as well as existing measures. Agreement on the application of these principles would enable us to establish a firm basis for implementing standstill/rollback commitments.

Over the longer term, our objective with respect to the establishment of effective disciplines over import restraints is to reach a comprehensive agreement on safeguard actions and achieve effective enforcement of GATT rules covering all other types of import restraints.

—Improving the MTN Codes. Five years experience with the agreements negotiated during the Tokyo Round indicates that there are a number of areas where improvements are needed. The United States seeks to strengthen the GATT nontariff barrier codes (subsidies, procurement, standards, etc.) by clarifying ambiguous applications and extending participation in and coverage of the agreements.

—Intellectual Property. The United States seeks an agreement on actions and procedures that will ensure that a proliferation of individual country practices in the areas of intellectual property does not act as a barrier to international trade. Trade in counterfeit goods needs to be addressed because it has become an increasingly serious problem and threatens to lead to an imbalance in the rights and obligations of contracting parties. Over the longer term, we seek to reduce trade distortions resulting from inadequate treatment of intellectual property rights.

II. Expanding Market Access.

An expansion of access to world markets is necessary to ensure that international trade and related investment increases for all countries, thereby facilitating economic growth and development, and helping ease foreign debt burdens. As tariffs have been lowered, there has been a more prevalent use of nontariff barriers. Negotiations on market access should aim primarily at eliminating such barriers. However, significant tariffs barriers also remain and we will need to analyze what creative new approaches might be considered in this area. The United States places particular emphasis on expanding market access for high technology products.

III. Investment.

New GATT disciplines are required for a number of practices not currently covered by international trading rules but which are nonetheless proving to be increasing sources of trade distortions. The

United States seeks to establish effective discipline over such trade-distortive measures as local content and export performance requirements. With respect to international investment, the United States would like to initiate a process leading to multilateral discipline over practices that distort or restrict international investment flows, including barriers to investment and other discriminatory measures.

U.S. Objectives for Negotiations Dealing with Trade in Services

Trade in services accounts for a growing share of global trade. This trade has taken on increased significance for all countries as a result of its critical role in fostering the application of new technology, which is central to economic growth. However, there are few international rules for services trade and no established procedure for negotiations that could lead to the liberalization of barriers limiting this trade. The United States seeks the development of a general agreement of principles and procedures to ensure that trade in services is as open as possible. Negotiations should be carried out by as many interested contracting parties as possible under the aegis of the GATT, using its administrative facilities and Secretariat staff.

Negotiations on services under the auspices of the GATT should aim at an agreement on a set of rules and principles for conducting trade in services. The agreement would be based on a commitment to transparency of practices and the resolution of problems through consultation. Procedures also would be established for the negotiation of commitments dealing with the reduction of trade barriers, including provisions laying out the nature of these commitments.

The general agreement on services should be complemented by negotiations aimed at the removal of barriers in individual service industries. We also forsee negotiations in functional areas, such as standards, as well as the development of an understanding dealing with investment issues in services. The United States also believes that priority should be given to developing a multilateral agreement on international information flows.

Appendix II

European Commission Statement of the Council Declaration on a New Round of Trade Negotiations, March 19, 1985

1. Suggestions for a new round of multilateral trade negotiations have been the subject of careful international consideration for the past two years. They received particular attention at the meeting of the OECD Ministers in May 1984, at the London economic summit in June 1984 and at the meeting of the Contracting Parties of the GATT in November 1984. Such multilateral negotiations have been a regular feature of the GATT since its inception.

2. The Council recalls that a new round, while of the utmost importance to a strengthening of the open multilateral trading system and to the expansion of international trade, will not of itself be sufficient to such purposes. Thus the Community, in the perspective of a New Round, and while working to achieve the broad consensus requisite for its launching, will urge that the following separate but related desiderata receive serious parallel consideration. Thus:

   (a) In order to ensure credibility, reaffirmation will be necessary of the international commitments variously accepted at the Williamsburg and London economic summits, and at the last meeting of OECD Ministers in Paris and of the GATT Contracting Parties in Geneva:

   —effectively to halt protectionism and resist continuing protectionist pressures (standstill);

   —to relax and dismantle progressively trade restrictions as economic recovery proceeds (roll-back);

   —to pursue the 1982 GATT work programme as complemented by the decisions of the contracting parties in November 1984.

(b) Solutions to imbalances whose origin lies in the monetary and financial areas cannot be found in trade negotiations. Determined concerted action is required to improve the functioning of the international monetary system and the flow of financial and other resources to developing countries. Results in the monetary and financial areas should be sought in parallel with results in the trade field.

3. Despite previous trade rounds, Japan's growth of imports of manufactured goods has nowhere near matched her export growth. Like concessions to Japan have not produced like results, and in consequence, an imbalance of benefits currently exists between Japan and her principal partners. It is therefore a pressing political necessity for Japan to bring her import propensity into line with that of her partners, by means of domestic structural and other adjustment as well as by measures at the frontier.

4. As regards negotiations on agriculture in the New Round, the Community is ready to work towards improvements within the existing framework of the rules and disciplines in GATT covering all aspects of trade in agricultural products, both as to imports and as to exports, taking full account of the specific characteristics and problems in agriculture.

   The Council is determined that the fundamental objectives and mechanisms both internal and external of the CAP shall not be placed in question.

5. On possible new topics for negotiation, the Council considers that trade in services seems suitable for inclusion. Problems of counterfeit goods and the defence of intellectual property also deserve consideration. Other possible new items should be examined on their merits.

6. The Council affirms the need for reciprocity and a better balance of rights and obligations as between all contracting parties. The Council considers that too selective an approach to individual negotiating points should be avoided. A balanced package of topics for negotiations should be agreed in which all participants will find advantages for themselves. In principle items should be negotiated and the results implemented in parallel and not in succession.

Glossary of Acronyms

AFL-CIO   American Federation of Labor-Congress of Industrial Organizations
ACTN   Advisory Committee on Trade Negotiations, United States
ASEAN   Association of South East Asian Nations
CAP   Common Agriculture Policy of the European Community
BIT   Bilateral Investment Treaty
EC   European Community
EFTA   European Free Trade Agreement
GAS   General Agreement for Services
GATT   General Agreement on Tariffs and Trade
GNP   Gross National Product
IBM   International Business Machines
ITO   International Trade Organization
ITU   International Telecommunications Union
LDC   Less Developed Country
LDP   Liberal Democratic Party of Japan
MFA   Multifibre Agreement
MFN   Most Favored Nation
MITI   Ministry of International Trade and Industry, Government of Japan
MPT   Ministry of Post and Telecommunications, Government of Japan
NIC   Newly Industrialized Country
NTB   Nontariff Barrier
NTT   Nippon Telegraph and Telephone, Japan's Phone Company
OECD   Organization for Economic Cooperation and Development
OMA   Orderly Marketing Agreement
OPEC   Organization of Petroleum Exporting Countries
R & D   Research and Development
SDI   Strategic Defense Initiative

SPAC	Services Policy Advisory Committee of the U.S. Trade Representative
TAA	Trade Adjustment Assistance
UNCTAD	United Nations Conference on Trade and Development
USTR	United States Trade Representative
VER	Voluntary Export Restraint
WIPO	World Intellectual Property Organization

Index

Adjustment, domestic, 4—5, 41; capabilities, 78; and growth, 28, 32; resistance to, 41, 66—69
Advisory Committee on Trade Negotiations (ACTN), U.S., 6, 62, 147—49
Agriculture, 39—40, 140—42
Antidumping Code (1967), 64
Argentina, 68, 71, 95, 102, 105
Asian or Pacific trade cooperation, 125
Australia, 128, 151

Baker, James, 7
Bandung Conference, 96
Bargains, cross-sector, 119, 139—40, 155
Bentsen, Lloyd, 63
Bicycle theory of negotiations, 6, 59, 74
Bilateral agreements on trade restraints, 21, 29, 41—42, 49, 67, 68, 121, 142
Bilateral free trade agreements, 126—29
Bilateral Investment Treaties (BIT), 121
Bonn Summit meeting (1985), 22, 87, 130
Brazil, 22, 34—34 n. 11, 68, 95, 102, 105, 110—11, 114—115 n. 6; informatics policy, 21, 29—30
Brock, William, 20, 21, 61, 68, 74, 93 n. 10, 130

Canada, 89—91; bilateral free trade arrangements with U.S., 90, 123, 126—28; and GATT, 90—91; provincial constraints in trade negotiations, 91, 127; trade, 89, 128
Canadian-American Auto Pact (1965), 90, 127
Caribbean Basin Initiative, preferential access to U.S., 126
Cartelization of industry, 29, 42, 68
Carter Administration, 71

Carter, Jimmy, 75
Chile, 105
China, 67, 95, 111
Citibank, 81
Coca Cola, 83
Commodities trade, 99
Common Agriculture Policy (CAP), 39—40, 79, 81, 133, 138, 140
Concession, 12
Congress, U.S., backing for new trade negotiations, 62—66, 73—74, 159—60, 162; Energy and Commerce Committee, 64; Finance Committee, 64; negotiating authority, 6, 62—63; and protectionism, 7, 59, 159; reciprocity bills, 120; unfair trade practices statutes, 25, 65; Ways and Means Committee, 64
Cooper, Richard, 16
Counterfeited trademarked merchandise, 51, 101—102, 149

Danforth, John, 63
Debt crisis, (LDC), 8, 98
Developing countries (LDCs), access to markets, 36—39, 98—99, 106, 108, 134; Asian NICs, 103, 105, 106, 109—11, 114, 139; and bilateral arrangements, 108; as a bloc, 95—102, 108, 110—11, 114; commodities trade, 99, 112; debt problems, 103, 105—106, 108; differing growth rates and prospects, 103, 104; and exports, 105—106, 109; and foreign investment, 100, 102; and GATT, 47—48, 96—98, 153; and graduation, 39, 97—98, 102, 103, 114 n. 5, 134; high-debt nations, 105, 106, 108—109; and industrial countries' adherence to GATT disciplines, 99—100; and labor migration to industrial coun-

About the Authors

C. Michael Aho is currently Senior Fellow for Economics at the Council on Foreign Relations in New York City. There, he is directing a multiyear project on "The Future of the World Trading System and the Challenges for U.S. Trade Policy." He holds a Ph.D. in Economics from the Massachusetts Institute of Technology and an undergraduate degree from the University of Michigan. Before joining the Council in 1984, Aho was the Economic Policy Adviser to Senator Bill Bradley (1983—84); Director of the Office of Foreign Economic Research at the U.S. Department of Labor (1978—82); and U.S. Representative to the Manpower and Social Affairs Committee of the OECD (1981—82). He directed the *President's Report on U.S. Competitiveness, 1980* and has published widely on international trade and labor market adjustment issues.

Jonathan David Aronson is Associate Professor of International Relations at the University of Southern California. He holds a Ph.D. in Political Science from Stanford University and an undergraduate degree from Harvard University. In 1982—83, Aronson was a Council on Foreign Relations International Affairs Fellow in the Office of the United States Trade Representative, where he was one of the principal authors of the *U.S. National Study on Trade in Services*, submitted to the GATT in late 1983. He is a co-author of a forthcoming book on trade in telecommunications services and of *Trade in Services: A Case for Open Markets*, American Enterprise Institute, 1984. Aronson is also the author of *Money and Power: Banks and the World Monetary System*, Sage, 1978.